T0339143

From a Year in Greece

BY FREDERIC WILL

Drawings by John Guerin

UNIVERSITY OF TEXAS PRESS, AUSTIN

The drawings by John Guerin were selected
from a collection made on commission from *The
Texas Quarterly,* and are used with permission
of *The Texas Quarterly.*

Library of Congress Catalog Card No. 67-20591
Copyright © 1967 by Frederic Will
All Rights Reserved
Type set by G & S Typesetters, Austin, Texas
First paperback printing, 2012
ISBN 978-0-292-75400-3
utpress.utexas.edu/about/book-permissions

FOR ALEX
*who will have
a Greece*

ACKNOWLEDGMENTS

I am grateful to the following magazines for permission to reprint from them, in slightly revised form: to *The Antioch Review* for "Athens; City of Dionysus," XVIII (1962), 65–82; to *The Yale Review* for "Mt. Athos," XLVIII (1958), 82–97.

CONTENTS

FROM A YEAR IN GREECE

Klagenfurt to Greece:
En Route through Jugoslavia

EN ROUTE TO Jugoslavia I spent my last night in Klagenfurt, southern Austria. That city announced the beginning of a new spiritual landscape: there was a different kind of country in the air. The onion church towers of southern Austria were part of the change. They suggested Russia to my unaccustomed eye. And there hung an unaccountable stillness over Klagenfurt, as though beyond it lay awesome landscapes: perhaps an infinite Sahara. So odd are the moods of Klagenfurt.

For a time I felt trapped. It was not so easy to pass into Jugoslavia; there was snow in the passes of the Austrian mountains, and I had first to cross into Italy, then to enter the Balkans from there. The stage was being set for a surprise. Even in northeastern Italy faces were bright, and the air flamboyant. A little of Rome in the air. The customs officials joked with each other. (Probably dirty jokes.) They smiled disbelievingly—now I understand why—when I told them I was planning to travel across Jugoslavia. Then before I knew it the Italians let the barrier down, permitting me to drive

slowly on. At once I realized that the road, followed easily to that
point, was changing to a pair of mud tracks. I was in Jugoslavia.

Two hundred yards ahead I saw the next customs-house, a small,
white building with another pole barrier before it. A few middle-
aged peasants were approaching the building on foot, leading cattle
and children: all seemed to be returning from work, presumably on
the Italian side. I watched them enter the place ahead of me. Then
I stopped the car and went in after them. It was cold outside: a
slight frost was still on the ground, and the air was damp. Inside,
everything was steaming from the meeting of cold bodies and clothing with the heat from a strenuous wood stove in the corner. I
found myself in a line, and waited, watching the thin, close-lipped,
cigar-chewing customs official. One by one the peasants went to
him, exchanging half-audible, friendly remarks, received stamps
in their permits, and went steamingly out into the gray air. I saw
them filing off down the road toward their homes. Soon I was
before the inspector's noncommittal eyes.

Thank God I had an irreproachable entry visa; I felt then, for
the first time in entering a new country, that my credentials were
under a mean eye. (This may be the rule in East Europe now.) The
thin man lacked the juice of humanity. In a quickly discovered mutual language, pig-German, he invited me out to the Volkswagen
for more careful inspection. I began opening bags, in an automatic
gesture. But the man wanted to be shown in his own way, to give
the directions. (What a wretched childhood he must have had.) He
looked over my piles of luggage, and asked to be shown certain bottom bags, keystones of elaborate arches. I complied with murder in
my heart. A first I was close to refusing. Then I sensed that the
whole trip depended on compliance.

In my possessions he found nothing of interest. Fortunately, I
was carrying only the boring private encumbrances of the body:

pants, ties, shoes. Disgustingly harmless. One of the last items was a wrinkled paper bag; the official saw it wedged behind the back seat of the car, and wanted it opened. He had been eyeing it with growing suspicion. I opened it: a pair of dirty tennis shoes. This broke his spirit. I was free.

Entering Ljubljana, a hundred miles into Jugoslavia, was like entering a city of the dead. I drove in at four in the afternoon, tired from a trip over poor roads, through demandingly unfamiliar scenery. Yet not all had been unfamiliar. At lunch I had ordered my meal in German: it was a little hard to believe I was in a foreign country. I remember the Jesenice *Sauerbraten*. And the handsome Buick—the joy of some great *Kaufmann*—which crowded up to my car in the restaurant parking lot.

But Ljubljana itself overwhelmed with strangeness. It seemed an empty city, so empty that I could feel no densities in it, that I had no idea when I reached the centre. On the main street, in contrast to the roads leading into Ljubljana, there were almost no cars. I wandered, almost drifted, down the street in my small machine. The roads were formally laid out, straight, wide, in good repair: rivers flowing through the city. The sidewalks wide, and empty. Occasionally, on a street corner, a person would be waiting silently to cross. In the background large plate-glass store windows echoed the emptiness back and forth. Over it all spread an uncanny twilight-orange glow. Not the lurid orange light which filters through an industrial city at night. Something softer and more final. It was an inner, sifting glow.

At the end of that first long street I began to study the house numbers. I seemed to be quite near the hotel where I hoped to stay: the hotel guaranteed by Baedeker. I looked closely, and was baffled. Where was the number? In the distance a man passed, stilly, slowly, inadvising. Another look at the houses. The desired number was not there. It existed only in the imaginary space between two present numbers, which met, wall to wall. The mystery with no solution grew. I was on the edge of a huge, open, concrete square, blocked on the far side, according to my map, by the University. More barefaced stone. A few more figures passed, like puppets across a scene as desolate as any painted by Chirico.

Then I turned back in the direction I had come, changing now to another street, to look for hotel number two. I found it, with difficulty. Searching, I realized how blank the façades of that city are, how many of them present only bare, vacuous, nameless walls to the street. (Like so many Masonic lodges in our own Middle West.) The Turist Hotel itself offered little more, only a thin-lettered sign near its roof, just over the third-floor windows. I took my bags and went in. Of that bare, clean, mediocre hotel no more needs to be said.

I went out for supper to see the city, or to find it. By now, although it was spring, a chilly breeze was blowing through the streets, tossing papers out of public trash receptacles and shaking the scattered lime trees planted along the street. It was five-thirty of a week day. The stores were closed.

When I came to the main street—Tito Street—along which I had originally driven, I saw people. There was no doubt of it now. There were many people, to right and left. But they appeared, in that first moment, to be frozen in groups. They were standing in clusters of ten or fifteen: almost no one was walking alone, looking in the store windows, or chatting with a single friend. Where were the pairs of lovers? After all, it was April. I walked down the street toward a group of young men, probably University students. Passing, I heard them speaking in low tones, seriously, as it seemed. (Though I didn't know their language.) There was little movement among them. Their faces, rapidly judged, looked pale and constrained. I was anxious to dispel the impression, and looked more closely at the next groups I passed. More of the first impression. Pale, static, constrainedly conversing groups stood before, but not looking into, the huge plate-glass windows of the stores. It was like walking through a circle of the *Inferno* reserved for the colorless, those condemned to an eternity of lukewarm conversation. No cars passed.

In the store windows the emptiness seemed to be prolonged, a kind of art-emptiness copying the real emptiness outside. (A ghastly twentieth-century mimesis.) Some commodities were displayed: in a department-store window were vacuum cleaners, and expensive household goods; elsewhere I saw "gift items"—leather and metal work; there were few clothes. Most of the windows had far more space than they needed. The objects had been arbitrarily displayed inside, merely dropped into the wide area. Again, as when I entered the city, the impression was of an abundance of formally limited but basically unused space. It was almost as if Ljubljana had been evacuated, and there remained only things in space. Things without inner organization.

Despite it all I found a *gemütlich* restaurant, as agreeable as any of my few Jugoslavian discoveries. Yet this experience, too, bore the Jugoslavian cachet. The restaurant was extraordinarily spacious: it extended far back into the block, on the ground level. There was an infinity of tables, few customers, and a low ceiling: all contriving to make me feel, as I entered, that I was penetrating the side of a mountain. I went to the depths of its chilly interior, and took a table near a radiant oven. At first I was nearly alone, again, and sat in proud silence examining my menu. Again a strangely familiar choice of foods. The German translation of the menu was semi-intelligible, no worse than the general run of such efforts.

After a while, when a good supper had done its warming, and I sat rather happily drinking a Jugoslavian wine, crowds entered the restaurant. I believe some of them had been among the groups gathered on Tito Street. This time, though, they were different; there were some lovers, some talkers, some talking thinkers. They sat at separate tables, two by two or four by four. It was good to see the smaller units. Some of the women were pretty, some of the men strong. It was a vital moment in the room, which seemed, even in its disciplined mildness—for this was not the left bank, even of the Danube—to be a haven in the empty, spacious city.

The distance from Ljubljana to Belgrade, by way of Zagreb, is about 350 miles. Theoretically the stretch from Zagreb to Belgrade is covered by the famous Autoput, a four-lane highway in good condition. (Actually, I found some fifty miles of it under repair, and was forced to take a nasty detour.) The whole trip, from Ljubljana to Belgrade, was moving and enervating.

Leaving Ljubljana is itself portentous. The only filling station in the city, that city almost without cars, is near the railroad station. I put my car in line for gas, along with several diesel trucks—the only other customers. As in Klagenfurt, there was again the feeling of being on the verge of a frontier.

Beyond Ljubljana lay rural villages in long, dull succession. They resembled country towns in Greece, though lacking some inner organization which gives unity to even the humblest collection of Greek houses. These Jugoslavian villages straggled a bit. Few people were to be seen in them. I drove painstakingly, both to see what I could, and to make the most of the imperfectly surfaced road. It took time.

In the middle of the journey, and on the edge of the much desired Autoput itself, lay Zagreb. My experience of it, regrettably, merged with the long spatial experiences that preceded and followed. Clearly Zagreb is a fine city. You feel, there, the battle between the old and new, a battle integral to Jugoslavia, which is in the grip of a political revolution that sets itself against ancient, untraceably rooted habits of life. The rectangular central square of Zagreb reminds of an agora, an ancient market place. Above it, raised by a stone platform, a market was being held in the shadow of a church. A number of matriarchal figures presided, hovering over trough-shaped cartfuls of oranges, lemons, melons, and an assortment of vegetables. It was a brisk Sunday noon. But many of the women wore light, tattered shawls, and soft wool slippers. They padded back and forth as though they were in their own homes.

The new also makes itself felt. In the big, prosperous restaurant at the end of the main square Germans and urbane Jugoslavs discuss political and economic matters. Occasionally a Ford or a Buick with fins draws up and parks ostentatiously. On the outskirts of the city rise new buildings, bare and institutional: government buildings.

But Zagreb was strangely forgotten when I left it to go farther east with the Autoput. The road was fine, seductively smooth. Having tanked up at the train station, I drove quickly and alone down the road and away from civilization. There were no cars around. I passed through the dull, quiet outskirts of the city onto the track through the land. No matter how modern such tracks become, encounters with them retain an elemental quality. Man reimmersing himself with awe in the spirit of the land.

Outside of Zagreb the country widened; I left the last southern spurs of the Alps, which had still been visible before Zagreb. The central Jugoslavian plain extended richly on either side of the Autoput. The fields were flat, and black, and in that spring the young crops looked vital. I was reminded, first, of long black fields in Illinois. By the time the difference came over me, I had reached a new part of the road, where, by imperceptible stages, the world became more desolate.

First it became flatter, perhaps not in reality, but in mood. Far away to south and north were long, low lines of hills. Their distant walls seemed to emphasize the flatness of the fields which I was bisecting: I was a point on a long, cutting line. At first the mood was peaceful, then I began to feel too greatly alone. It was perceptibly windy. The few trees which appeared, at a distance from the road, agitated their new leaves. The new shoots of the wheat fields —though those fields themselves were rarer now—trembled lightly. Getting out of the car for air I found the wind blowing coolly up my sleeves and biting my ears. Turning around I gradually realized how alone I was. From the human standpoint, at least. There seemed to be no axis for me in the things around. Nature was far away, and yet it was all that was, absolutely embracing. The world was still.

I drove on. The involvement with nature grew steadily more complex, as though I was driving toward a still center of the world, an unexpected matrix in nature. There were no cars, no houses, no birds, few trees, just the spirit of everything. Before long, a speck grew to visibility as straight ahead as the arrow-eye could see on that accurate, endless road. It was a speck or a drop of ink. It grew like the kernel of a storm. As it came nearer I saw it was a car, but not the usual car. And yet the shape and the motion of this car were average. Soon it passed, bearing an unsmiling functionary. It was even a government car. It was a radiant car. I gathered it deeply into vision. It was an artifact, a symbol of man's mind, and in it, in fact, was a man, a so-called human being. It was a missile from the human community, and I watched it vanish as if it were a ship leaving me on a raft. Then I understood how alone I felt.

I entered Belgrade in the rain. The suburban streets were badly lighted, and there were cars parked treacherously along the dark curbs. The air was black that evening. At one point I drove straight over a traffic island, which rose like a huge checker at the middle of an intersection. That half-frightening, half-comic event made a strange mood stranger.

I came suddenly out of suburban Belgrade onto the centre of the city. At the top of a hill I found lights, the neon climax of a big city at night. Before me was a hotel, the Moscow; one of the best in town, according to Baedeker. I nudged the car into a nook on the crowded street, and went in to inquire. The language was still German. Yes, they supposed there was room. (I later learned that there was a great deal of room.) Going out for my bags I noticed the marble columns in the lobby, and the high-style, formal furniture. My bags were brought in.

Almost immediately I went out to eat: after the trip on the Autoput nothing seemed important but food and sleep, in that order. The restaurant was even barer than the one in Ljubljana. Only a large, austere picture of Tito decorated it. Except, that is, for the elaborate lesser appointments—florid light fixtures and gilded woodwork, which only increased the weightiness of the bare walls. The food there, as in the Jugoslavian restaurants south to Greece, began to take on a generally "Balkan" character: pilafs, big green salads, coarse dark breads, yogurt. It was late, and only a few people were there. Stillness prevailed in the big room. I went back to the hotel through light rain.

The hotel was nearly vacated by this time. Bright lights shone down from the high ceiling, making the marble columns and the marble floor gleam. The large, empty pieces of furniture were placed massively around the walls. At one end of the lobby was a bar; all the stools before it, except two or three, stood like lofty toadstools unoccupied. The bartender busied himself ineffectually, much like the hotel clerk; when I entered, the latter was engaged in a heated argument with an underling.

I went upstairs, and found my room again at the end of a long walk of shabby, rose-colored carpeting. The lights along the corridor were dim. Inside the room, it was dull too. Now that the sky was black outside and the corridor dark, the shabbiness of the room was painful. First I noticed the bedspread. It was wine red and dirty looking (though no real dirt was visible). It was of a smooth cotton texture, but some of the fibres were tattered and stood up like hairs or tufts of grass from the fabric. The wallpaper was rose colored and peeling, like badly sunburned skin. Again the single lightbulb in the ceiling spilled a faint, barroomish flow of light. I walked in leadenly, worn-out.

From the window, before I went to bed, I looked out on the bright, central Terazije Square of the city. It was a long, oblong area of business offices and large stores. In the centre were benches. It was impressive: the partly meaningless signs, blazoned in yellow and red on the impenetrable, raining night. They underlined the alien quality of the place. And on that tone the day's consciousness would have ended. Except for the unfixable dripping faucet in the bathroom, and the leaky toilet. I slept long but interruptedly.

Two daytime experiences in Belgrade bear on all this. My intention, on this trip, was to travel through Greece. I was not sure of the best automobile route south from Belgrade. In a smartly appointed, state-run tourist bureau I asked for advice. Should I drive

by way of Pristina or Niš? I watched the face of the pretty girl who
advised me. She said it didn't matter, the road was equally good
either way. Several promising brochures were offered, luring to
Byzantine and Moslem sites along the routes. I went out pleased
but suspicious, and planned to visit another bureau, which I did.
There, from a responsible looking, middle-aged man, I had the
same answer. The roads were all good, he said. There were places
for stopping along the way—hotels and inns. So, even though the
serious-minded Baedeker had stressed with asterisks the difficulties
of the car trip south from Belgrade, there seemed no reason to
hesitate. There being, furthermore, no alternative.

The sequel, and therefore the point, of these tourist-bureau encounters in Belgrade will follow shortly. To anticipate, the roads
south of Belgrade, to the Greek border, proved to be very bad, and
the accommodations along them equally bad. It was a hard, almost
harrowing trip. It is clear that the tourist agents in Belgrade misled
me. It is nearly incredible that the government's agents sent me on
my way so full of illusions. This event came to take on a general
meaning for me later. It symbolized something empty and false in
Jugoslavia, something which, in the nature of things, must be only
a part of the picture.

In that vein, I mention the effect of Belgrade's official, govern-
mental architecture. Like most official thought, the public buildings
in Belgrade are rigid, formal, massive. They lack character. There
is more to be said, though, about Belgrade's aesthetic effect. Some
of the chief edifices there—such as the post office and the parliament building—are impersonal and sham even beyond usual expectations. Their façades look like cheap stage settings. Their stone is
cold and soulless. The lawn of the parliament house was unmowed
and weedy. Doing business in the mammoth post office I felt like a

puppet. Or an insect embedded in marble. I looked at the people who passed as if they too were simply that. So pernicious is the effect of the official, public sensibility.

The first half of the first day's driving south of Belgrade was agreeable: I passed through an unexciting, gentle landscape. The few towns met were busy and decent looking, some almost idyllically "Balkan," with painted carts, and women in colored kerchiefs. I stopped for lunch at Kragujevac, where I ate again in a huge, spacious restaurant. Now I remember chiefly the busy, kind waiter, and the filthy floor. There was a potbellied stove at work in the middle of the room, and I sat near it. I also talked, in a way that from this perspective seems highly charged, about how much farther I should go that day. At that time, among interestingly strange faces and sounds, the day still seemed to have an indefinite horizon.

The second half of the drive south from Belgrade was hard. It is impossible to convey that difficulty in mere talk of roads, weather, and accommodations: but those were the external ingredients of suffering. South of Kragujevac came the first signs of a breakdown in the highway. It was still a two-lane road. There were still only a few cars. I still preserved conventional notions of what a road is and does. But mile by mile, in the flat, poor, agricultural landscape the road degenerated. From cement it became asphalt, in several gradations. Great cracks, often broad enough to swallow the whole base of the tire, opened across the road. The edges of the road shaded off more and more noticeably into the land; the road threatened to become a real track. This last threat was at least symbolically disquieting, even from the start. It opened a vista of the struggle of civilization with nature, a vista which was at the same time being rapidly closed by the blunt necessity of more careful driving. For the road soon changed from asphalt to dirt surface, a stony, tan dirt, which lay like the icing of a cake across the land. It was most irregular in width, varying perhaps from ten to thirty feet. Usually it was broad, though. In my small car I wandered rather aimlessly back and forth from one side of the road to another.

To the steadily worsening driving situation, the weather added furious complications. By three it was cloudy, by four it was raining, in a slow, confident descent from the accumulating clouds. Some mud oozed across the road, like living, primeval slime. But worse were the potholes which quickly developed; the road eroded away from the rocks embedded in it, leaving toothlike projections in one spot, and crisscrossing arroyos in another. The car pitched and rolled, alone on the broadening sea of the road. By late afternoon, as it began to grow dark, I grasped how far I was from any plausible destination for the day. Ten miles an hour was maximum speed. The land was alone with me again.

The few towns through which I had been passing seemed to have no accommodations, certainly none I would have chosen. These towns were small collections of small houses. Each collection had a muddy main street, which was lighted now by a string of dim bulbs, each doing its ineffective part in fighting the dusk. Most of the houses were sunk in an ocean of twilight, as though they were only parts of some cosmic dream into which everything was dissolving.

By seven it became imperative to stop wherever possible. I was exhausted. The rain had been heavy for an hour, slamming persistently at the windshield. For some time I had been following a truck —the only other vehicle seen for two hours—up and down the hills. It was a dark night. Beyond the glow of my headlights and dashboard I saw only the moving spot of the truck's tail signals.

Eventually, still far off in a valley, a cluster of lights appeared. It was Vladicin Han. I knew I must spend the night there.

There was clearly only one hotel in Han: it appeared on the right, at the end of the main street, just as I was beginning to lose hope, or rather to invent desperate schemes. The Turist Hotel was dimly illuminated and old; from the outside it looked like a converted barn. I walked through the rain into the front door, and saw to the right the occupied but shadowy restaurant which covered most of the ground floor. Everyone looked alike just then, to my first, tired glance. They were all men, all dressed in black (or brown) peasant clothes, all moustached, all involved in what sounded like local gossip, as they sat at their meals, or their drinks. At that moment I felt strange, and longed for a language to reach these men with. I spoke in German, which was of almost no use now, and managed to get the proprietor; he inspired no confidence, but made it clear he had room.

The day ended in the narrow room to which I then carried my luggage. It was a cold room. The bed was low and dingy, like a pauper's coffin. I shut the door, longing now even for the pretentious elegance of the Moscow. It had been an afternoon of immersion in maleficent nature; a number of concentrated circumstances had joined against me. Against so much external difficulty, internal rebellion was inevitable. My body (and nerves) struck back at the day with a night of tremendous illness. I was glad to come through it all.

It was a long day's trip from Vladicin Han to the Greek border. I rose to this trial after a desperately hard night. The day was blessed, though it began cold and gray. Light all around me was the finest imaginable setting for existence. I strode in it as though it were a solution of pure vitality. By six that morning I was in the car. I felt vastly relieved within five minutes of departure from Vladicin Han. I breathed.

The ambient nature was now precisely that of the preceding day. It was quite as monotonous, at least at first. The hills were humped and low, the continuous plains falling away flat for some two hundred yards on either side of the road. Soon I was utterly reinvolved in the gravity of landscape. Hardly before (now obliterated) Skopje, the first goal of my drive, did the hills start to climb, faintly suggesting at their tops those mountains which strongly divide Jugoslavia from Greece.

Skopje itself made no advances through charm, though I saw it, too, with clean eyes. A real city, of minarets, Turkish quarter, and harem atmosphere. (Although, the papers reported at the time, a vast Communist program of modern building was underway there.) Skopje was the first substantial collection of human beings I had seen since Belgrade. Yet there was no air of vitality. Few cars, slack and saggy waiters in the dirty hotel where I ate, unkempt streets and lawns. Only an impression, but a strong one.

South of Skopje the mountains climbed, and I entered the deep, cutting valley of the Vardar River, which I would follow nearly all the way to Salonika. It was my guide through the rock, and I followed it down toward the Mediterranean like those first Hellenes who went the same way to Hellas, earlier than 1500 B.C. Did they feel something of the Aegean in the air, and follow it?

There is little more to tell of that southward journey; I include it all in the final encounter with Jugoslavia, at the border customs-office, and in the first encounter with Greece, at its border station. To that drama now.

The Gevgelija station is far more elegant than the point where I entered Jugoslavia. I saw it several hundred yards ahead of me, a modern if small white building on the left. There were a few cars

parked around it. The windows were clean and open. Ahead I saw
the barrier; beyond was the similar-looking Greek border station.
I stopped, unaccountably anxious.

In the Jugoslavian station was an air of mediocre officialdom.
(Preferable to the air of my first customs-office in Jugoslavia.)
Here all was impersonality and dispatch. The men in civil servants'
uniforms came forward, checked my papers, looked briefly and dis-
interestedly through the car, and raised the long pole barrier as un-
questioningly as if they were raising their national flag. I hardly
realized I was changing countries. (Borders only exist if they are
felt.) The shock was momentarily delayed.

I drove through the nationless strip to the Greek house. I was
tired. It was just after noon, and the preceding night was beginning
to tell. I went into the bright room: Realm of Greece. Intuitively I
was at ease. The men in green uniforms were sitting informally
around the room, chatting. I understood, as usual, forty percent of
their language, though it had been two years since I had heard a
word of it. Now I had to speak it. In front of a short, handsome
man with amused eyes I inventoried my luggage. Efforts at speaking Greek delighted him. The rest of the men in the room listened,
fascinated. I guess I was an unusual apparition at that northern station. Soon the officials were questioning each other about me. It
came out that I had been married in Athens, six years before. The
men were delighted, amused. One of them asked why I had no
children. I was in Greece.

To complete this spiritual change it was only necessary to enter
the dining room annexed to the customs-office. I am not ashamed
that the spiritual climax of my Balkan passage occurred in that restaurant. I was alone in it with only a buxom pair, the owners, who
showed me the choice of foods and then served it up. They had a
refrigerator full of good fish, *barbounia*. There were cheeses and

ripe olives, cold artichokes in oil, fish pastes, good dark bread, and melons. A nice wine was ready, too; Dionysus' greeting. I sat and ate and drank.

Eating, and looking out over the green, gradual hills which sloped to the south, seeing birds moving almost stilly in the air, I thought freshly of how good the things in the world are. I thought of the commitment through joy which I really had to the land, the earth itself. Now, at the far end of a long road, the land, and the things grown in it, seemed to rise willingly toward me, to offer themselves.

"When I Was Bringing Horses Over from Larissa": Northwest Greece

NORTHERN GREECE is crowned with a significant city, Salonika. Except for its Acropolis, even Athens would be less than Salonika. Athens is ringed with profound, bare hills, but it lacks a closely complementing ocean. Piraeus has ocean, but remains a commercial port. Salonika has both a good harbor and an active urban culture in the same place. It is part of its own world.

The sense-binding, sense-shaping ocean is omnipresent there. It is visible from nearly any point in the city. You only need to go up to your second story—if you have one. There is that pure, rhythmic, bounded but boundless element, spread somewhere at the bottom of the street. The same vision glimmers or stirs at the end of nearly every east-west-running street. Many townsmen spend much of their time promenading along the harbor. They seem to be subliminally magnetized to the sea.

I spent several weeks there. During that time I would often go up to the crowning Venetian walls, and look down onto Salonika and its harbor. From there Salonika's deep dependence on the ocean became a fact proved by eyesight. The city is built on the half-moon-shaped plain of the Axios River. Two images came to me repeatedly: that Salonika is an amphitheater facing the ocean; or that she is a lover, reaching to embrace the ocean. Here are the hot, white (or cream-colored) buildings of the city; there is the element they thirst for.

The ocean spread a dazzling floor. I used to watch it by the hour. A restless network of colors, ranging from turquoise, close to shore, to deep sky blue farther out, and exchanging positions and tones ceaselessly. Nothing could have looked cooler or purer: the sea looked the opposite to hot, dusty, dry, mortal Salonika. Yet there was a counterimpression, of a unity in the picture. I formed the impression that the Salonikans have found their own image in that sea.

The nights in the city confirmed me. Where did their power come from? After dark a tremendous life awoke in the streets. I would go out to walk on the broad King Constantine Boulevard, beside the ocean, just as the coolness of the sea came onto the land. There I would find myself swept into the crowd of walkers, as they surged back and forth, talking strenuously, shouting, laughing, gesturing.

From the beginning I had thought: this surging of people resembles the surging of the sea. It has the same rhythmic energy. If it were day and I could go up to the crown of the city and look down, I would see this pullulation of humans interweaving like the waves just beyond them in the harbor.

I had thought of the origins of man in the sea. Maybe the rhythm of humanity and sea at Salonika harked back to a primal kinship. The people of this city may have found their unique way back to the beginnings. Remembering, in the surge and weave of their walk, the cool nights when their first ancestors were rocked

and woven in the depths of the ocean. This remains my essential
thought about Salonika.

In a way the thought was too essential, and the city too concentrated. One morning, on little more than impulse, I left Salonika at
dawn by the road to the west, and before long found myself, after
the heat and dust and power of the city, in the midst of the freshness of nature. There were long fields of grain full of poppies, ap-
ple and pear orchards just beginning to bloom, and always the
mountains, several of them clearly seen and rising not far from the
road. I was astounded to see how much snow was on them: against
the watery blue sky that morning they looked powerful and massive. Not craggy, like Alps; but more rounded and accessible. Greek
mountains.

Those scenes made an impression which is hard to describe. Yet
at the time, they wanted to be described. It was almost as though
there were an independent will in the land. I would get out of the
car time after time and look around carefully. I felt a need, almost
biological, to find words in which to digest the experience. In the
present telling it sounds "precious." But it was not.

Adjectives came to mind as leitmotifs: that morning the world
was pure, innocent, whole. Words like that were some help. But
they didn't join together, like words in a good poem, to create a
whole image. If the mood could have been transmuted into ideas
without destroying itself—which was doubtful—I would have
said: In that pristine context I was stirred by an original nature
which was the counterpart of self. And which caught me sweetly
into itself.

As the trip began, so it proceeded, offering a tableau of nature
which seeped in. In this pervaded mood I readied myself, I see now,

for the second wave of the rural invasion; for the meeting with Demetrios and Aleko.

That famous event took place early in the afternoon, ten kilometers from Florina. There, by the road, I saw two men, usual enough in appearance, who gestured me to stop. They wanted a ride into Florina: one even showed his card, to prove that he was a policeman. I took them in gladly, and with an innocence surpassed, as it turned out, only by theirs. I had no idea yet what hitchhiking would come to mean.

At first there was little to say. Standard questions. Where was I from; where going; what was my business; was I married; did I have children? Why not? (That query was part of the canon.) I looked over from the steering wheel to the policeman. He was intent on my face and answers. Of course I was to accept my central role. I did.

As I answered I tried to think. Why do Greeks stare, absorb, drink the strangers? It was a puzzle. I played with a theory. If all people acted naturally they would do just what those men were doing; they would absorb strangers. This is a primal, animal hungriness which is the basis, if not the perfection, of love. Among sublimated people this trait is suppressed: being more complex and problematical in their development, they sense the delicacy and complexity of other selves like them. This awareness leads to sensitivity to the privacy of those other selves, and to a desire not to intrude. The Greek mood is more naive and more profound. The theory went out on that note.

In the company of such attentive friends I reached Florina, a northern-looking town near the Jugoslavian border, surrounded by high hills and low snowy mountains. No tourist town. The central square was bleak, the architecture hopelessly dull. Yet it was no surprise when the two friends insisted on showing off the high spots. They lived in Florina. They were proud of it, and anxious to have their home admired. This was payment for the ride; it was forced on me strenuously.

We visited and visited. First an agricultural farm, where English pigs, Greek chickens, and American cows were housed in friendly unity. I was introduced widely and taken around by the head of the school; in the process meeting its members, and answering flocks of questions which I had already fielded for the hitchhikers. It was something of a delight, at that point, to see my two old friends answering the questions for me, publicly proving their possession of the stranger.

From the farm we went to the cemetery, where we looked at the graves of soldiers who had fallen in the Greek Civil War. One of my friends had been schoolmate to many of these fallen. He point-ed out the graves of the men he had known. On one there was a poem, written by the man himself from the hospital where he died. The poem was a kind of autobiography, climaxed by the sentiment that his life had been well spent in the defence of freedom. All this I looked at, and felt. The mood of the moment was full. There we stood, outside of town on a rocky, windy hillside, in the freshness of nature. All was caught in naturalness. My friend spoke of his dead friends, but with no sentimentality. Across nations to me, whom he had met only a few hours earlier, he was reporting on the violence of existence. Death seemed resolved and purified here; the look it assumes on ancient Attic grave markers.

After that we visited a hospital. The chief institutions of Florina —farm, cemetery, hospital—were appropriately concerned with fundamentals of existence: raising of animals for slaughter, then for food; human death; human illness. Florina is a fundamental town.

But the picture I leave of it is still too sombre. It was fun being

with Demetrios and Aleko. After our tour we went for coffee. Time
was forgotten. We exchanged addresses, made plans to send books
to one another, and discussed politics. Above all we smiled and
smiled at one another over the marble table in the coffeehouse. A
good moment. To be followed by even a better—the moment of
picture taking.

We should all be photographed together: the three of us, each
with a copy for eternity. In the main square of every Greek town
are several photographers waiting to take (fairly crude) pictures
and to develop them quickly. We went. I have the picture now as a
memento of our simple, oddly assorted group. I stand in the centre,
looking hopelessly American; nearly a foot taller than my friends.
They flank me, moustached, happy, straight backed, Hellenes to the
single long fingernail on each hand. We are all radiant with a
rather nervous pleasure at this culmination of our acquaintance.
Love is visible under the strain.

To it I add, from this later date. The innocent and whole nature
I found that day among mountains, poppy fields, and wheat was
akin to the nature of those Florina friends. The purity of my new
acquaintances rose out of the deepest stratum of human nature, at
the level where it is closest to the nature outside us. My friends
were in close touch with their existence as sense-beings.

From Florina to Kastoria is a hard drive. The mountains, high
and laid at disorderly angles to each other, make the road dip and
wind interminably. But the time passes, amid ragingly beautiful
views of valleys and of ringing, snowy mountains. It is a hard,
infertile stretch.

This inundation by nature was pacifying. I look back on it with
special gratitude in view of what followed; the hectic encounter
with Kastoria. I approached that city by night. It glittered up from

far below in its valley. I was freshly astounded, on seeing it, by the daring of men in cutting towns out of nature, in establishing themselves broadly all over the land. I have seldom been so struck by the humanity of man, plain Homo sapiens, as I was at Kastoria.

The layout of that city is unforgettable. It is banked against a high hill, which dominates an almost encircling lake, a deep, energetic lake fed from all sides by the mountains. The town of Kastoria itself is not quaint or intimate. But it has a distinctive air of culture. I was surprised to discover, in this present-day center of a prosperous fur trade, houses and churches which had been raised in an aristocratic age.

Kastoria has seventy-five churches. Of these most, I understand, are small and elegant. The six I visited were just that. The elegance and profusion explain themselves historically. During the Turkish domination of the city, in the four centuries preceding the Greek War of Independence, many citizens of Kastoria were imprisoned by the Turks. Certain of these Greeks, in their imprisonment, promised to erect chapels to the Virgin if they were freed. Many did so: built chapels of gratefulness adjoining their private houses. That was the great age.

Times have changed. The age of America has reached the city now. But the Kastorians take us in their stride, not in ours. I learned this at the Greek-American Institute.

That Institute is a private organization devoted to the teaching of the American language to Greeks; it has branches throughout the country. Its teachers are either native English or American speakers or Greeks with a good knowledge of our language.

The teacher—the only teacher—at the Kastoria branch was Demetra. She took on hundreds of students, held classes from two in the afternoon until ten at night. She carried—I hope "carries"—on the work with unbelievable vitality. I met Demetra, who introduced me to other people. Before day's end I had met most of the town's younger generation.

This is how it happened. Demetra didn't work in the mornings, and she loved to speak English. (Having lived for several years in England.) So she volunteered to take me on a morning tour of Kastoria. Thus I happened to visit six of the private chapels. Thus I met most of the inhabitants under thirty. They flocked around Demetra.

The city is built on a hillside over a lake. As we went uphill, or along the lakeside, young people from ten to twenty-five would appear in doorways or at windows to speak with "teacher." They would ask her about the American, exchange gossip, or recommend sights for the tour. I saw what a centre of energy she was: of good height, with the expected black hair and restless eyes, and with a surprising intensity. She showed me Kastoria with strangely objective pride. (A quality of unprejudiced passion which is rare in Greece.)

After the trip we found ourselves, in company with a number of the people met along the walk, reassembled in the bare reception room of the Greek-American Institute. It was time for lunch. They —all the suddenly come friends of Demetra who had brought contributions for the meal—sat around, flirting, laughing, questioning. And offering me, in voluptuous sequence, pieces of meat, bread, apples, almond cookies, and, at the last, more than enough crème de menthe.

After lunch they put me to work. It was one-thirty, a half hour before the beginning of school for the day. Demetra asked if I would help with some classes. I nonchalantly agreed; consultant on the English language. (Too much crème.) I took my seat among the pupils, who were in their early teens. The lessons were exuberantly handled. Recitation, writing on the board, joking: all in fair

English. All with great verve. Students asked me questions, too: I remember only one. *Q:* Do you think Greek girls are pretty? *A:* Extremely. *Result:* Delight. Laughter.

Later it was my privilege to teach a class alone. It was five in the afternoon, and I was feeling tired. But by then it was time for the advanced *Gymnasium* students: the oldest and most serious group. A good deal was expected of me, and I did my best. But Demetra wasn't there, at first, and by some fatal urge I fell to discussing politics, Cypriote politics. I observed the students in front of me. Clear-eyed, serious, good-looking. Simply American college freshmen who happened to speak a different language. I soon returned to my senses. Nationalism flashed. The sky blackened. Anti-British convictions, drunk in at the nipple, flowed on the air. I briskly changed the subject.

The intense life of that Institute was evident again after the class. It was six-thirty. In the reception room the young students of the seven-o'clock class—all girls—were gathering. They seemed to know very well who I was. (I am sure the whole town knew by now: people had looked at me on the streets, already that afternoon, as though they knew everything about me.) These girls were, I suppose, between thirteen and fifteen: talkative, naive, pretty, curious. They questioned me into the unwelcome role of distinguished foreign emissary. (The sort of situation, I suppose, about which the State Department is always cautioning.)

In that group I answered a hundred questions. Not the usual ones about myself, but the usual ones about America. About its climate, history, geography, and people. On a map I pointed out where I had been born, had lived, where our capital is, and so on. The vitality of those girls is unforgettable. It still gives me strength in weak moments.

I left them, the Institute, and Demetra that evening, and Kastoria the next day. But little is forgotten from the experience.

I left early in the morning, wanting to reach Meteora that day. I would not have minded an easy trip. Instead it turned out to be the supremely testing "day of the hitchhikers." Two groups of them were memorable; I mention only those. In all, though, I carried about twenty hikers, in five different groups, before bedding down at Meteora that night.

There is nothing remarkable or heroic about that transportation service. I bring it up to suggest, in a new way, the almost epic naturalness of Greek countrypeople.

Most of the people carried were clearly excited by the ride: for many of them it seemed to be the first auto experience. For instance, two women whom I met in a small café, where I had stopped for directions. The road was poor, and I had to decide how to go to Meteora. At the decisive crossroad stood a block-shaped white café. I went in and immediately found myself the object of fascinated attention.

After handling the first questions—which included advising an old man about the desirability of his emigrating to Australia—and eating a plate of fried eggs, I looked around. The room was small and dark, but slowly I saw. There were some fifteen people around me, watching closely, impatient for me to finish and talk. There were a couple of soldiers, a pair of shepherds, several owners of the café, and the two women.

One of the women was fairly old: a strong, wrinkled farm woman dressed in black, the standard color. She was forty kilometers from her home—the town of Grevena—and was urgent for me to take her and her daughter along. Grevena lay on the Meteora road. The daughter, an intelligent, lively, rural woman of thirty, seconded hopefully. The whole café was suddenly full of urging. As though I had considered refusing: rather I threw myself into the general mood, became delighted, more than I could quite naturally be, at the solution of the women's problem. Well filled with coffee and eggs I went out, and we set off down the winding, stony road.

During the trip the two Greek women—who were either actively or passively sick most of the way—said little. They sat together in the Volkswagen's narrow back seat and looked miserable. I longed to be alone. Forty kilometers took a long, long two hours.

At our destination I thought the social obligations would be over. I had misunderstood. The two women climbed stiffly out from the back seat with their battered luggage. They thanked me, praised me, and invited me in to dinner with them and their family. I refused, as politely as I could in Greek. Then they ordered me in. While the whole emerging family, pouring from the house like the first creatures from the ark, sizing up the situation instantly, joined in the invitation. I was helpless. Surrounded by husbands, aunts, grandparents, and a baby—all of them welcoming me and the returned women—I entered the house.

Coming into Grevena I had taken it to be the poorest sort of Greek village. The surrounding land is dry and rocky: the sun shines hard there. The town itself is simply a spread-out group of square, white-stucco, one-story houses connected by irregular, dusty roads. From the outside, who could guess at the spiritual juiciness inside those houses?

The house was dark and small. The mud walls kept it cool, too. All of us found seats, fairly jammed together, and the men began chatting while the women, except for my two tired passengers, attended to the meal. My powers of Greek speaking were badly strained, although of course everyone listened with fascinated sympathy to my simple remarks. Greeks have endless humanity: they judge the man wholly by his spirit, not by his form.

At the meal I was offered the best of the house. Two kinds of meat, an aged white wine—uncommon in Greece—a large salad, good fruits. By then I had gotten used to the tapestries on the walls, the simple divan and chairs, the intent faces. We drank toast after toast to one another. A young, recently married scion of the house, in his early twenties, kept reaching his glass over and clinking it against mine. The meal went well.

Afterward we all sat together. My former passengers, who were by now fully restored, looked beatifically at me. I especially remember the older: black hair framing her large eroded face and her intense eyes. On her ears small golden earrings. Briefly, her peace seemed to be my peace.

The next stage of the "day of the hitchhikers" had no focus. It was a brief, chaotic moment, impossible to recollect in tranquillity.

Some twenty kilometers north of Meteora, as I was crossing a green valley in midafternoon, I saw fifteen little boys walking in the road ahead of me, in the direction I was going. They were returning from a soccer game, and were kicking a dusty soccer ball along the road as they went. It was a great surprise when, just as I was nearing them, they ran out into the road in front of my car, and forced me to stop.

I looked at them closely. Like many Greek boys, they had swarthy aquiline faces, bright eyes, and well-formed, shaved heads. They were quick and instinctively fearless in motion. I called out: get away, leave me alone! They swarmed over the car.

I opened the door and asked what they wanted. It was simple. They wanted me to take them some two hundred yards farther down the road, nearer their homes. As I saw how cheerful, if insistent, they were, I agreed to take four of them—three in back, one beside me. I said I would open the door and let four in. No more allowed.

When I opened the doors, of course, the car was flooded with tense bodies. They climbed behind the back seat, lay on the floor, and sat three-deep in each others' laps on the seats. It was touching, and I almost hated to do what I did next: to remove them by the collars, one by one, until only four remained. The entire transaction was peaceful. The boys were not surprised; I was not angry. Justice had been done.

I remember the wild scene as we five drove off: the defeated ragamuffins laughed and waved at us from the roadside; while the lucky four, whom I was saving from a walk of two hundred yards, looked disdainfully back at their friends. They were the *grands seigneurs,* not I. For two hundred yards they had the hard-earned pleasure of considering me their chauffeur.

The so-called Meteora (the up-in-the-air things) are twenty-four monasteries. They are perched like birds' nests on the needle-shaped, low mountains which lie just three kilometers from Kalambaka. Those points of mountains, which lodge the monasteries, merge farther north into a solid mountain massif.

On first approach to Kalambaka I saw nothing on the needles or fingers of mountain. The rock is red-brown, nearly the color of the monasteries. It is hard to notice forms—rectangles or cupolas—there. But the closer I came the more form appeared; the more hint of culture in that nature. With a kind of intoxication—it was a strong mood—I finally saw monastery after monastery perched on the crags. The intention of the first monks here, in the ninth century, had been to cut themselves off from the world; at the time they succeeded. The only access to the monasteries used to be by baskets pulled up and down by ropes.

From first sight, though, I knew that the original intention had been fulfilled in *only one sense.* The Meteora may be isolated from society, as they are still today, but they are profoundly imbedded in nature. I realized this during my night at the largest monastery, Ta Meteora.

During the afternoon of my arrival I had visited—driving over the bending roads from tip to tip—the now three chief monasteries and nearly the only ones still inhabited. It had been depressing. There is little wealth now; a few of the chapels are sumptuous, but nothing remains of the usual Byzantine treasures except a few crowns and candelabra. The remaining monks, perhaps a dozen at all, are lacklustre and uninspired.

After my tour I had returned to my room in the bare but comfortable guesthouse of Ta Meteora. The room was whitewashed, clean, and simple: it was full, just then, of reflected sunshine. My only window was to the east, and I went over and sat in the big sill of it. Sunset had come quickly, and had already transformed the surroundings.

The grass just outside my window was fiercely green, seeming to radiate a light inside it. A few poppies were equally on fire; as though incandescent heat, flickering in their stems, had turned the petals to flame. Across the abyss before me—my window faced straight out to the east from the point of the needle—I could see Hagios Stephanos on an adjoining crag. That huge building was ruddy in the sunset, and just the color of the rock it surmounted. Nature and art were blended there. I could see, scattered about over the other needles, a half-dozen more monasteries. Each seemed strangely to be melting into the peaceful, fiery landscape. While far down in the valley lay Kalambaka, surrounded by green plains, and set astride the long, dark Peneus River. That landscape had a peacefully eternal mood: like the backdrop of a painting by Memling.

It was while sitting there, in spirit a part of that mood, that I realized how fully the Meteora—the things in the air—belonged to nature. I seemed to be returning with the whole scene, via my senses, to nature. Only a few objects of wealth were left to the cloisters. Only a few souls to preserve them. The buildings needed repairs. The vital spiritual undertaking was being returned to the nature it sprang from. In a sense nothing is stronger than a blade of grass.

Trikkala is some thirty kilometers east of Kalambaka, farther down the green valley of the Peneus. It is an ancient city, the birthplace of Asclepius, and the heart of the Greek hinterland. I found it, like Salonika and Kastoria, a center of uncanny vitality. There the resemblance stops.

Trikkala is unique. It revealed its self to me in two ways. The first was open and public; but the second was secret, a discourse of essence.

There is nothing more public than the bazaar at Trikkala. It is an open market, several square blocks in area, laid in the centre of the city. It is open daily, and in it everything is sold. Lambs, fish, buttons, saddles, figs, dresses—all are sold there. The merchants are as various as their goods: old shepherds in jodhpurs and black cloaks; wrinkled, shouting market women in black dresses; wizened, canny little girls who have come for the day from the farm; slick, city merchants noisily displaying fabrics or kitchen utensils to the country people. All is noise, color, smell, movement. Even in the great bazaar of Istanbul there is no vitality of this kind. Only in Crete have I seen such proud, stern men or such haughty women: in

Trikkala, somehow, they are more authentic, less conscious of themselves.

I could see that this bazaar was important to me, and I walked up and down it many times. There was a mob. Women buying, men talking, surveying brassware or saddles. In general the men and women stayed separate. And wholly intent on whatever they were doing. Only in Trikkala, of the cities I know in Greece, was I —as a conspicuous foreigner—completely ignored. That city is absorbed in its own life.

In its secret revelation to me, Trikkala made this point clearer. It was during my noon meal, on the main street of the city. After walking around the bazaar I had gone into a large, clean, white restaurant. It was already nearly full, mainly of business men and merchants from the bazaar. There was enormous talking, a forest of gesturing hands, and one empty table toward the centre of the room. I took it.

Before long I had a cheese omelette and a glass of beer in front of me, and was settling into the noisy but somehow peaceful mood of the place. Gradually, though, I became aware that the loudest sounds were localizing themselves at a large table near me. From mouthful to mouthful I would look up, until finally I became fascinated, as others seemed to be, too, by the six old *pallikaria*—manly devils—who were sitting at that table. I couldn't tell whether they were quarreling or joking together. They spoke fast and loud and excitedly.

On the marble table where the *pallikaria* sat were large carafes of resinated wine: the men were drinking it out of shiny, copper cups, and were emptying the carafes fast. As I listened closely I gathered that the talk was about horses. The men looked like shepherds: black cloaks, jodhpurs, high black boots, florid black moustaches. One of them was telling how he had lost some horses, and seemed to be accusing another—opposite him—of stealing them. They weren't really angry, though. The others contributed steadily to the argument.

I looked longer, and the raucous laughing and joking from the table slowly became thunderous. The *pallikaria* were completely unselfconscious. They had no interest in the effect of their talk, which was considerable. As a group they were totally caught up in the excitement of conversation. Everyone else in the restaurant seemed equally caught up and delighted.

The last image I keep from that moment is clear. The six have grown very excited. One accuses another and is furiously—but half playfully—rebutted. Fists are beaten against the table top, fingers shaken in faces: they are enjoying it thoroughly. Two new wine carafes are brought. Momentary silence follows, until the largest of the hefty group—a "character" to judge from the way the others treat him—starts on a story. "A few years ago when I was bringing horses over from Larissa . . ." Everyone in the room listens. And, as he goes on, I am forced to think of a swarthy Odysseus, who was much driven after he had sacked the holy citadel of Troy.

Oleanders and Olives:
Aetolia and Acarnania

COMING FROM THE northeast I drove slowly. The day was long and easy. I was rather lost in myself, I guess, when I saw Ioannina. It came gradually over me that I was looking down toward an oasis, a handsome settlement on a hill overlooking a lake. The road from Trikkala led through the Langada Pass in the Pindus Mountains. That high gap—the highest roadbed in Greece—is often snowy and misty even in spring. I had understood, in crossing it, why the Pindus range is the main barrier to east-west travel in Greece today, as it was for Caesar's men. The descent from that height toward Ioannina was long and tortuous, through foothills which gradually lowered until at last the city came into sight. At first it was hard to accept the existence of the plain with its blue lake. I saw the road, far ahead, circling the lake and slowly disappearing into the edge of Ioannina, like a snake entering its hole.

In the plain, the calmness of the lake imposed itself. On the water lay Ali Pacha's island, inviting, a little weird, like a romantic poem's enchanted island. I could just make out a few small churches among the island's heavy trees. Even Ioannina itself, to

the moment of entering, refused to look real. There was greenery
on every side of it, the fields were un-Hellenically fertile, and the
houses seemed large and prosperous.

These impressions remained intact, and that is the mystery of
Ioannina. The city was still and dignified, not grand. In spirit I
found myself continually drawn from the place toward its lake, re-
posing in placid, almost languid beauty, a kind of beauty rare on
the Greek mainland. The main square was beside the lake. The
major roads led down to the lake. The Turkish *Kastro,* with its
high fortifying walls, and mosque (minaret intact) hung over the
lake. On the still island, in fact, much of the active history of the
city has transpired.

It was there that Ali Pacha, the Turkish administrator of Ioannina in the late eighteenth and early nineteenth centuries, had his
private residence. That hated, colorful man retired there regularly
with his mistresses and his counsellors; while the intimidated Greek
residents of the city whispered nervously about his habits. Ioannina
still seems to be turned whisperingly toward the island, as though
toward an unforgettable, inerasably scandalous memory.

Yet even the island is still now. Rather, *it* is especially still, sunk
in its own memories. Taking one of the small boats from beside the
main square of the city, I arrived at the island within ten minutes.
Ioannina receded swiftly, until only the façade of the old Pacha's
palace, with the trees below it, was distinctly visible. I found myself in a village of small, chiefly pastel-colored houses, and stone
streets.

Through and around the village stood small churches, several of
which were founded in the thirteenth century. Their histories were
various, made crazy reading. Around Pantaleimon are the cells of
former monks; inside the church is the spot where Ali Pacha was

killed, in 1822. The nave and apse themselves, there as at the other churches, are miniature, only large enough for some fifteen worshippers. The walls, even with their complete covering of frescoes, are dark and the air chilly. At the opposite side of the village, in the tiny monastery Ton Philanthropinon, are powerful sixteenth-century frescoes. I saw a life of Jesus, and paintings of ancient wise men. The woman who opened the church recited the names of the works passionlessly, then left me alone in the dim chapel. No prayer had been heard, no incense smelled there for a century. Stillness swallowed my eyes until the forms faded, and I moved uncertainly toward the door and the sunlight.

The silence of Ioannina and its island seemed borrowed from the surrounding land. That lightly populated, and contentedly fertile land appeared to draw its inhabitants down into it, into its own placid mood. Ancient ruins are as passive, there, as anywhere in Greece.

Nearly twenty miles from Ioannina, at the end of a drunken but passable road, I came on the ruins of Dodona, the cult centre dedicated to Zeus, and famous in antiquity for its oracle and its prophets. The first view of the remains was tinged by impressions of nature. There were hills, rising in some places to mountains, on every side. On their lower slopes were authentic pine forests, rare in Greece (or anywhere), and fields of tufty brown weeds and wild flowers. Poppies were conspicuous, their heavy heads blown by any breeze among the rust-colored grasses. There were no houses to be seen: the nearest village was several kilometers.

The remains of Dodona are extensive, but sadly dilapidated. There is a theater with an acropolis above it. Some private dwellings for the priests, and several temples, lie in the sanctuary. Though Dodona was a smaller cult centre than Delphi, it was active longer—until the fourth century A.D.; good proof of the long survival of ancient religions. A large number of unidentified but evidently "religious" buildings have been found. Among their ruins, figurines and pottery have been dug up. The small adjacent museum contains many of these objects.

But there was little material evidence to help the imagination feel its way into the mood of ancient Dodona. What little I knew from literature helped to establish the mood. The Selloi, priests of Zeus, were the chief power there. They divined the god's will from the motions and sounds of the talking oak of Dodona, that tree which, like the sacred palm on Delos, or the olive tree of Athena on the Acropolis, had supernatural power. Though there are no more oaks at Dodona, the spirit of the story still summons the place. To me, even nature seemed articulate there. Even that stranger story, that the Selloi walked barefoot in order to "hear" the commands of Zeus through the earth, was helpful. It dramatized the feeling, so strong at Dodona, that everything natural is articulate, and that the entire complex of buildings was originally constructed out of a sense of the union between nature and religion.

I found this union easily at Dodona. The mood of the land itself, particularly its confident, whole stillness, seemed to have won at last. The god and his priests had been drawn back into the fertile earth. Even the excavated buildings showed only their eroded foundations above the consuming ground. Yet the earth was not malign there. Rather, to return to the ancient image, the earth seemed to express itself at Dodona like a mother who has benignly sent forth her children into the world, and has embracingly received them back. As mother, the earth is the source of belief, of whatever unchallenged confidences in reality we can still enjoy. Magna Mater, in her still bounty, is the mother of religions.

I touch only two remembered and meaningful features of Arta: each, in its way, returns me to the question of that city's strange peace. Yet, before more is said, a qualification. The centre of Arta bustles. The main street is lined with small shops: paper stores, grain stores, fruit shops, butcher shops—all intermixed in rapid succession. There is great motion from store to store, as determined housewives swagger down the narrow sidestreets swinging their filets. Donkey-pulled carts clatter by in the street, carrying sober farmers. There is calling from windows, noisy bargaining in the shops.

In the middle of this vitality are found many nooks of shadow and stillness. These may be large, cool cafés with small business. Or so it seemed. I would come upon them at the several squares of the city. The cafés were dark, except for the disk-shaped marble table tops, by which I would guide myself on first entering. A few older men would be sitting around over coffee and newspapers, but there would not be the mob of dice throwers and backgammon players evident, for instance, in Trikkala. A busy-mannered, white-coated waiter generally presided. The café was a kind of haven.

There were abundant trees in Arta, too, spreading a shadowy peace on many small streets, and over the benches in the squares. In those squares a person could sit and watch, enjoying the sun's force in the form of beauty, not of heat. Even in some of the shops this was possible. Many sheep bells are made and sold in Arta, generally by craftsmen whose forges are at the back of their shops. In their long, crowded, musty establishments it is cool—unless the forge is blasting—and withdrawn. As I passed along even the busiest streets I would notice shopkeepers in the still recesses of their property; cool, all-watching spiders.

Not all the peace in Arta was built at the centre of the bustling town. The outskirts—seldom more than five blocks from the main street—ran off into open country, and took me into corners of the town where, they are so still, it seemed that no life had moved for centuries. A strange ante-bellum atmosphere in those streets, like a waft of South Carolina. Of course there was nothing Georgian. The houses were stucco, one storied. The lawns were small. Dried fruits were strung at some windows. The streets were narrow and un-paved. The flowers did most to set and hold the sensuous tone. Oleanders spread in profusion beside the houses, trailed onto the dirt road, and perfumed the opaque sky so as, oddly, to accent its visible intensity.

The Church of Saint Theodora lay at the end of one of those back streets, nearly submerged in white, and red-white, oleanders. As it approached the church, the street narrowed, becoming little more than a path. That narrowing of space before me, as I walked, coincided with a thickening in the air, and a concentration of the flowers' visual effect. There was the feeling of walking into, to-ward, an indefinable sensuous center. A small gate divided the road from the precinct. I opened it, and went in. Luminously, the church flew against my eyes, driving them back with its brilliant white walls. No church in Greece is so luminous in the sun. In that gleam-ing air the flowers, even on the sides of the church, hung still, held. Birds, scattered across the air, were still, perfected. I was seized, almost immobile, in that instant where the intense silence of Arta gathered.

Amphilochia, at the southeast edge of the Gulf of Arta, is of relatively small historical or cultural importance. It is not unusually

"picturesque" or alluring to travellers. Yet it has a private quietude
—for in western Greece you must distinguish by kinds of quietude
—which demands attention.

That whole region's isolation and closeness to nature were especially apparent in the drive from Arta to Amphilochia. That trip
rounded the east line of the large Gulf of Arta, which spread blue
and mild to the west until it emerged through a small out- (or in-)
let into the Ionian Sea. The Gulf was like an inland lake: its
strange stillness was, in fact, attributable to its almost landlocked
situation. To the east of the road there was rising land, hills or
bluffs coming down to the roadbed. I felt half pressed down toward the water and toward the flatter land.

Amphilochia lay on that flatter land, at the south corner of the
Gulf, just where I seemed to be leaving the world of water. The
Gulf curved, and bent up to the main square, before which it spread
itself like an offering. A narrow *quai* stretched forward from the
city like a finger testing the water. The sidewalk around the periph-
ery of the square was slightly built up above the Gulf's level; something made me wonder, from the start, what it was like here during
storms. The houses stood back with reserve, watching the Gulf
from their terrassed positions on the hill above the square. The
ruins of a fortress topped the hill. Fairly standard equipment.

Along the protected side of the square there were shops and restaurants. The latter large and bare—except for the metal tables—
and, like most Greek restaurants, innocent of the least elegance. I
entered several, examining cuisines and bubbling pots; and examining refrigerators for choice fish. No secrets were made. I remember an infinitely deliberative old man inspecting the flat, penny-
eyed lake fish piled in a refrigerator, then asking to have his meal
brought to one of the tables in front of the restaurant. The harbor
square lay still and surrounding as he waited for his meal.

That gulf, like most inland bodies of water, was capable of brusque attacks, and equally sudden reversions to passivity. In the middle of my meal I noticed that the water was stirring, at first superficially, like land showing the initial slight agitations of a volcano. Small waves appeared, fanning out like wrinkles. Quickly the wrinkles became furrows. A breeze blew itself up, and with it a few thrown sea drops. They were salty; the thin outlet to the sea was ocean. (This water may have come from the New England coast.) The sky quickly turned darker, overrun with tumbling clouds. Suddenly even the water was gray-black.

In the gradual agitation of water and air there was excitement, though the town lay indifferent, and the square was empty. Food had strange savor, my senses opened up inside me, tasting the world as they seldom do. Inner alertness grew with the excitement of the Gulf, which had soon thrown a few gallons of water into the middle of the square, where wetness spread itself slowly across the gray stones. There was still no one around: at most a hurrying child, apprehensively going home, or an old woman running an errand to a meat market. I finished my meal, paid, and walked carefully across the wet stones to the outer promenade of the square. It was slippery. The air was clear in my nostrils.

The spray was thrown casually across the stones. As far as I could see over the now completely nervous gulf the water and the sky met in a single, seething grayness. A lonely instant. But the turning point, almost tangible to the instant's mood, came promptly. Nearly imperceptibly the jets of spray began to recede. Simultaneously there was a faint alleviation of the sky, the air growing both cooler and quieter. Then the arching of what had come nearly to be waves, at least lake waves, hesitantly lowered itself. The stirrings in the water fascinated me with the light reflected in them. The air grew clearer from within: looking up I found the sky a radiant,

still-unbroken veil over the sun. The sun was poised, placeless, omnipresent, on the edge of vision again. The terrassed town waited. The world hung in stillness.

Stillness adopts many forms in Greece and those especially finely differentiated in the western part of the country. I have mentioned some of the distinctions. The stillnesses of Dodona, Ioannina, and Amphilochia differ from one another. Yet I suppose all stillnesses are one through an underlying power of awakening meditative harmony. Agitation alerts human being, forces it forward onto the threshold of its existence. Silence holds us in musical wholeness. This was the thought of those mediaeval mystics—Täuler or Eckehart—who wrote of total silence as the state in which God addresses the soul. They appeared, in fact, to believe that the attainment of the right silence was an invitation to God to address us, to break our silence.

Missolonghi enjoys unique silence. The city is built on marshy, salt-pit land at an inlet of the Gulf of Corinth. The entire area is flat and lonely, with few trees and everywhere the smell (not always good) and feel of water. The climate is unhealthy, somewhat malarial. In this virtual desolation—". . . cette ville misérable, triste et malsaine," says the *Guide Bleu*—Missolonghi stretches itself over a wide area. Its buildings are low and white, unusually homogeneous in appearance, and stationed stiffly along the broad, regularly laid-out streets. The characterful silence of desolation hangs over everything.

There is also discernible, to the visitor acquainted with military history, a depressing temporal weight in Missolonghi. It has been a city of one main doomed enterprise. Before 1822 it was an insignificant town near the swamps, known only in its region. In 1822 the Greeks made there, quite unwisely, one of their strongest stands

against the Turks in the war which was to result in Greek independence. The Greeks quickly found themselves besieged. Lord
Byron, as all know, joined the group of assailed men at Missolonghi in January of 1824, and shared their increasingly hopeless situation until his death there from fever on April 10 of that year. The
others remained until, in 1826, the long Turkish blockade obliged
the defenders to abandon the city with great loss of life to themselves. In 1828 the Turks surrendered Missolonghi without a shot;
but even that satisfaction has not dispelled a mood of still discour-
agement from the city.

Little in Greece, in fact, is as joyless as the small bust of Byron
which stands near his grave, in the yard of a public school. The
head is without inner life, and at the same time romantically un-
pretentious. The street and sidewalk before the school are hot; the
sun bakes the town to a pure silence. Byron seems, for once, little
more than a sad memory. Even the formally disposed flowers,
around the school walls, are thinly existent. You are, here, deeply
inside the distinctive silence of Missolonghi.

Not far west of Delphi lies Amphissa, to which I came subdued
from Missolonghi. Amphissa is not without its genuine "objective"
interest; it is surmounted by a *Kastro,* a walled fortification which
was in the fourteenth century both Frankish and Catalan, and which
is now a romantic ruin with extraordinarily competent murals; a
bazaar runs smack through the centre of the town; and there is, as
from Delphi, a superb view down onto forested hills, then valley,
and finally onto the Gulf of Corinth with the mountains of the
Peloponnesus visible in the background. Most moving to me, somehow, was the town's location: among olive groves.

Coming from the west I tired of the winding road long before it or I reached Amphissa. I was hardly conscious of the first appearances of the town. From a distance only the *Kastro* was visible, and even that thickly shaded by trees. It was necessary to lose this first sight in several more windings of the road before reacquiring it, somewhat more distinct. White houses, parts of a main street, some details of the *Kastro* walls: all these could be fairly well distinguished. But the dominant impression was of the olive groves which surrounded and veiled the town, revealing it only by the chance of breeze-blown leaves.

The southernmost part of northern Greece, as it nears the Gulf of Corinth, seems to be a steady dropping-off toward the water. From Amphissa to Delphi, for instance, I drove on a road which had been painstakingly levelled against the downgrade of the hills. Amphissa stood on a terrasse set against that kind of downgrade. Around it on that terrasse, as well as above and below on the hill slope, spread the olive groves. They hemmed the town with distinctive peace.

The olive leaves were dusty silver colored on the underside, dark green on the upperside. Their evanescent appearance was caused by the continual movement of the surfaces of the leaves. Any breeze was able to turn them. Silver and green, they changed positions against an opaque blue sky, so solid and close that the leaves seemed, from a distance, to touch the blueness with their motion. The sun prevented the scene from being too heavily colorful. As often, this Greek sun was colorless, a placeless, formless energy filling the sky until everything under it is spiritualized from the inside. Amphissa itself lay in peace under this sky and these groves.

Its peace was guaranteed by its olive trees which, seen from a distance, turned lightly, hotly in the day, but seen from below stood cool and protectingly against the day. Amphissa was guarded. The day filtered through to it only as beauty, or as a sun tossed fragmentarily across an opaque sky. The ground under the trees was damp a few inches down. Its recesses were utterly still. Amphissa itself seemed to be shrinking away from the sun, back toward such recesses, with almost an imprecating gesture, and the remark: ". . . my stillness is the most complete of all."

Athens: City of Dionysus

I HAD BEEN almost a month coming from Germany, and was getting tired of travelling. So I did little justice to the country around Delphi, or to the Theban Plain. I turned my Volkswagen busily across that territory, which I had, in any case, seen before.

I remember clearly what it was like to pass Delphi, hastily and by car. Nothing brings home the twentieth century more plainly than putting on the brakes beside, and getting out for a drink from, the Castalian spring. How the Muses must shudder at those encounters. But I took courage from the strange familiarity of the scene. Delphi is odd that way. All the old sights were there to a glance: the Apollo temple; the row of treasuries; the stadium at the top of the compound; the circular temple below; and, far down, the Gulf and its boats in the sun, and beyond it the excruciatingly beautiful lavender mountains of the Peloponnesus. It seemed to have been no time, literally, since I had seen it all. And remembering it, as I write now, I seem again to hold the place in a puzzling timelessness.

I left it behind me with what at the moment seemed like impiety, but remembers itself today like one of those rapid greetings permissible only between long-time acquaintances. Twentieth-century velocities encourage these moods.

Anyhow I was soon onto the familiar road leading by Arachova, Livadeia, and Thebes. A few years before, I had covered much of the territory, and much more closely, as a student working out archaeologically from Athens. The beauty had stayed, though now I passed more quickly. Fatigue, seeping farther into me with every bend in the road, had no force against the aesthetics of the experience. Olives, oleanders, cliffs of pine, immense prospects onto the Gulf, back toward Missolonghi, down the Peloponnesus toward Patras or Corinth, towns carved whitely against mountains; these attacks on the senses were too much for a Puritan. I stopped whenever I could, beside the road, trying to assimilate the beauty.

Coming down onto the Boeotian Plain, after Livadeia, was a relief. Since Salonika there had been unremitting mountains. This country really *was* a hunchbacked giant thrown up from the centre of the ocean. Suddenly I was down on earth again. I passed Askra, Hesiod's Vermontish rockpatch farmland, and came into flattish Thebes at dusk on a clear chilly Thursday. The streets were lined with *kapheneia* and *taverna* business. Strings of electric lights. A good many men playing checkers and dominoes while wives and daughters fixed dinner somewhere down the dark side streets. I pulled up at the Tourist Hotel.

I remember almost nothing from that night. There was an ordinary enough meal—pilafi, some wine—in a bright, loud nearby restaurant, maybe a short walk before dinner. I slept hard in my room, sharing it with some travelling salesman, then rising very early, before—as I believed—he had even been very long in bed. I had paid the night before; now I went out into the first, chilly streaks of dawn.

As I started out of town I saw a needy hitchhiker beside the road, and in spite of myself pulled over. Even from a distance I saw that this man was thin and lame; and from closer I could tell that he was shabby. When he turned, I opened the door. Somehow there was no room for mistrust.

In a minute he began to talk. It came out in a flood. Everything we passed was a fountain of discourse. Behind these trees he had hidden when the Communists came down on his town, near Thebes; he had shot from a hole in that mountainside, when the enemy went down this highway in trucks; his sister had been killed over there. I didn't understand nearly everything. His conversation was too fast, and of course too committedly intense. But what I didn't hear I supplied from observation. His face was dark, even as the day lightened, and his features were mobile, adopting a series of expressions in almost ritual succession. First he would frown, then grind his teeth angrily, then—as the particular anecdote reached its climax—he would open his mouth rather wide and emit a mirthless laugh. I would answer briefly, then let him go on. I'm afraid I grew quickly to have little feeling for the man, one way or another. Meanwhile we passed into Attica.

I digress onto this gentleman from Pindar's city only because I shared, and unexpectedly, with him. It was now nearly sunrise. The rose streaks had taken an hour and a half to grow into bands of light, then finally to coalesce in the intenser fusing light of what promised to become sun. We were perhaps an hour from the outskirts of Athens; still on the far, north side of the range which separates Athens from Boeotia. There was no other car on the road. We began to climb. Silence in the car.

At the top of the Parnes range I could tell that excitement was ahead. The air seemed held, and as though about to escape and utter, articulate. At some astounding turn in the road the whole sky

exploded red before us. The road was drenched with sun like a
running yolk which flowed down into the valley, then into the
plain, before us. The sky was azure invaded by rose. Down at the
end of it, where the road ran into the horizon, was Athens. Itself
a myth. The life-labored fellow was crying at the sight.

It would almost have been better, in Athens, to have known no
one; to have taken that city, for three months, straight and whole
and man-to-man. As it was, I spent much time that fall and winter
trying to be alone, not so that I could see what I hadn't seen before,
not so I could *spy* on the city, so to speak, but so as to test older
impressions and, of course, to have fun.

I got in the night habit again quickly, though it had been almost
lost to me in the three preceding years. I would eat my dinner late,
then go to one of the little *tavernas* around Omonoia Square. Sometimes I would read there, or write a few letters; more often just
exercise the joints of my stiff spoken Greek. I began to get inter-
ested.

Many of the Omonoia *taverna* tables seemed, in a way I'd not
realized, to be altars of a subterranean Dionysiac religion. There
was some ineradicable ritual blooming here. The wine and dancing
were different now, in our day. I could see that. Modernity had
some meaning here. But who could say that the ritual was different?
I took this question home with me often. It teased, though it didn't
worry.

Thinking back now it comes to me like this. On a typical evening the dancers would be soldiers. Several of them, in separate
groups, would have come after dinner to the Nuktopoles to drink
wine, eat cheese, and talk; probably arriving late, after ten, because
the music started then. The *taverna* would be almost affectedly
casual: four instrumentalists and the singer all eating before they

enter; then emerging from the back of the *taverna* chewing, and walking through the warm, low-ceilinged basement room to the band stand. Neither the soldiers nor anyone else—the lovers or the chattering old men—would pay much attention. Probably the customers see nothing piquant in the stubby, breasty woman who will sing, or in the assortment of mustached men who begin to tune up instruments. So it would seem. Yet I add "probably": it is always hard to know what the foreigner thinks of his own people.

Greek soldiers are cliquish. At each table—on this evening—they talk gaily, excitedly to one another. In one sense they act like school children, trading gossip, joking naively. Like school children they are exclusive; sitting in the *taverna* with them you feel oddly shut out, more even than from most Greeks. You have to see these men in action to understand them (and the world, I guess, knows from the last war how understandable the action of such men can be). Not long after the musicians enter, the soldiers start tapping their boots on the wooden floor. Outside, perhaps, Ford taxis are blundering by. From nearby Omonoia Square there may be a muffled noise of the Saturday-night crowd, the single sound made by a horde of individuals. But inside, a more precise rhythm begins hesitantly to form itself from table to table like the still-distant, growing conversation of drums in the jungle. The soldiers are speaking to one another.

The third piece to be played is, say, a *syrto*. The *bouzouki* is the dominant instrument now. It is a four-stringed guitar, from which distorted and passionate notes can be twanged. For leading hard-stepping dances it is perfect; the other instruments are violinish strings and perhaps a clarinet. The *bouzouki* bears the thread of passion like an electric wire. The soldiers rise to its sounds, and by tacit consent the other customers draw back from the centre of the room, leaving a space for dancing. It is reminiscent of the orchestra areas in those earliest Greek choral dances, areas that were to be stages for tragedy later. Now with the naturalness of children the defenders of Greece gather in this basement *orchestra,* making themselves a chain of held hands. For a moment they test the chain's strength, flexing and relaxing their arms. They are handsome on this verge of their *syrto:* short, strong, olive-complexioned, as though their tough, favored fruit had become the substance of their skin; then they move together.

The *syrto* is a weaving-line dance, led by a man at one head of the line. (Is he a newer form of the *choregos,* who led those early choral dances and became the first actor of tragedy?) The leader holds by a handkerchief to the man next to him, for a reason not immediately apparent. At first there is simply a single current in motion, through the line: several steps to the right, fewer to the left, then a pause, then onward, in solid, emphatic time to the rhythm. The rhythm is potent, a kind of coronary violence. The clientele has turned to the center now; a few clap their hands in time. At last the leader leads.

Wrapping the held handkerchief tightly around his fist, he lets himself go into a squatting position, stamping the while. He is a living, flexible piston. The other links in this wild-headed chain move obediently around their core rhythm, following the leader as he bobs up, moves farther, squats, and stamps echoingly with his heel on the hollow floor. The man preserves grace, with violence. His motions are as disciplined as those of a ballet dancer. He sings inside his movement as the stuff in a good sonnet sings within its form. Even if you don't know the pattern of the *syrto,* this man brings you the feeling of its form. Everyone is tired when *he* finishes, in an orgy of hopping and sweat that brings applause, in its final stages, from the discerning audience and renewed efforts from the lanky, puffing *bouzouki*-man.

Standing about afterwards, the soldiers smoke, laughing among themselves or with the musicians. One of them flirts with the *chanteuse*. One of the clientele sends up a decanter of resinated wine for the men, and they drink it down fast, smacking their lips. While the mood of the event is heavy in the air you think it over. The dance has been sudden. It is not that these soldiers are entertainers, here to entertain. They emerged from the group of the public, the you. Do you want, though, to pass public-spirited judgment on them? Saying, for instance: "How good it is for soldiers to occupy themselves so, rather than in brothels or bars." The comment rings false. All such thought is banal, but here it is especially out of place (whether true or false). This is not a hearty good time these men enjoy. There has been something demonic in the restaurant. You pour yourself more retsina and think: Dionysus is here.

During those months I thought frequently of Nietzsche's dictum that Dionysus is not a Christian god. I remembered that Dionysus' followers are never respectable; that they never sit at deliberations of the UN or try to improve social or economic conditions in their communities. They are, as we say, un-American. We, members of a Western society, worship Christ, not Dionysus. (Christ is dangerous enough.) Perhaps every person retains a Dionysiac side, a wine-drunken twinge in some nook of his being. But collectively we disapprove and even disavow.

It occurred to me seriously, that winter, that Dionysus still lives in Greece, and in the best health. This despite the widespread effort, in Greece itself, to stamp him out. Many agencies were contributing to the effort: the Orthodox Church; the pro-American government (Karamanlis); the conspicuous pro-Western faction among the intellectuals, so many of whose training has been in

western Europe or America. Even the common people, whose relatives were in America to make money, and frequently failed, were
contributing. The commoners heard the news about the "States."
Then they tried to bring the thoughts and moods of our fast-paced,
mechanized society into their own existence. The things of our society were slower to come, in fact have not yet come; Buicks and
Bendixes come later; in the beginning is the Buick mentality.

The Greek effort to eject Dionysus was slow and far from suc-
ceeding, or so it seemed to me. I began to wish either that it would
never succeed (preferable) or that it would succeed quickly. The
transitional efforts resulted repeatedly in falseness. I saw pretentiousness over and over again in Athens—in the manners and ges-
tures and words used to exorcise the demons of the Greek blood,
and to lead the people into finer ways. The swankiest hotels of
Athens showed this pretention to a beautiful degree. They catered
to the foreigner, and forsook the brethren. For example the help in
those hotels had become eager to please western Europeans, and,
above all, Americans. But not Greeks. Humbler fellow Greeks—
unless they were the cotton-raising type from Egypt—were looked
down on in such fine establishments. In foreign countries Greeks
may cling to one another like blood relatives—I have seen it in
America—but it does not happen in Greece. No country—not even
ours—has suffered from a crueler civil war than Greece after the
Second World War. The Athenian's sometime hatred of his fellows goes hand-in-hand with a flattering attitude toward the foreigner, particularly toward the powerful foreigner. I hated to be
reminded of this. Where there is a domestic perversion of nature, it
can always be found to have some public form. This kind of domestic perversion let itself be seen in many fashionable Athenian
hotels.

The pretentiousness of such hotels seemed to me to lie in a conscious effort to turn the back on the Dionysiac spirit of the land, toward the more "enlightened," disciplined West. Elaborate and usually ludicrous efforts were made to speak the language of the clientele: French, German, English (according to the political situation). The foods served in the dining rooms were Westernized: roast beef, ice cream, rolls; foods no Dionysus ever ate. The prices were astronomical, out of any relation to the Greek scale. The appointments were floridly western-European, or eclectically "modernistic," with a generous use of plastic and chromium. Nothing could have been less authentically Greek. Even the public lavatories were carefully designated by the non-Greek symbols: *W. C.*

In fact such pretentiousness—fear of the Dionysus in the blood —seemed to have invaded the entire question of the use of language; to have descended into a fundamental form of existence. This is serious. Extreme solicitousness to speak the foreigner's language was already a symptom of the invasion. When I read the untranslated menus in the hotels I understood better. And even better if I bought a conservative newspaper from a bellboy. It was sure to be written in a vocabulary and style reminiscent of fifth-century-B.C. Attic. There would be few of the words which I was used to from daily conversation or reading in Athens. I was, in a word, reading that form of modern Greek known as the *katharevousa glossa,* the purified language. Dionysus never spoke it. Now only the diehards uttered it. But it was the language of hotels.

I saw then clearly that the *katharevousa* I read on the menu in the fanciest Athenian hotels, or in the royalist papers, was a dying and pretentious language. I could recognize the deep paradox in the contemporary linguistic situation of Greece. Linguistically, modern Greece must find itself in its own way. The Greek language has to grow away from its ancient *form.* And that it is doing. Yet modern Greek is part of a long linguistic tradition and must do its growing out of a language matrix. The matrix, in this case, is great and fertile. It must, or should, be used without concession to pretense, or mere form. Mere form is the worst crime against Dionysus.

If Dionysus speaks *demotike,* the language of the people, he does it nowhere more loudly or unpretentiously than in the street markets of Athens. One of the longest and most vocal of those markets is on Sophocles Street. (Athena and Hermes streets are also full.) In fact, the Sophocles Street emporium—which I passed every morning on my walk—is simply a long line, on either side of the street, of private shops; their wares generally displayed on the open sidewalk. Standing alert for sales the shopkeepers shout to one another, peer to peer, or call to anonymous assistants circulating through the backs of the shops. Obscene, hearty, aggressive camaraderie is the spirit of business here.

Actually, little seemed to be sold on that chaotic street. I kept my eye on it, but seldom saw a customer. Most of the transactions were wholesale. Yet the goods were displayed as they would be in any retail store: bags of various commodities, waiting to be examined. Grains predominated. There was a steady, dusty haze in the air from the tossed sacks, dropping with their dry barley, oats, wheat, flour, peas, beans. Thud after thud, the donkey-drawn carts or the small trucks bringing up their wares, then leaving.

Business began at eight in Sophocles Street; though the street is narrow, already at that time it was crowded with an almost entirely male crowd. (Only a rare Moll Flanders invaded the gathering.) I tried to walk down the street and found myself dodging obstacles, abandoning the sidewalk, then guarding my steps in the cobble-stone street. Every time I raised my eyes from my feet I walked into the streetcar rails and stumbled. Whenever I looked too closely at

any of the men by their shops, someone darted quickly across the street just in front of me. I became obsessed, deafened, stirred up by the street. The best tactic would be to stop by one of the *koulouria* vendors, on one of the street corners, to munch a crusty, dry ring-bun, and to watch the scene at leisure.

The farther I advanced down Sophocles Street—and I experimented often—the more deeply involved I became. This walk repeatedly transposed itself into spiritual metaphor; it was like the mind's progress into the inextricable jungle of Thomism, which at every stage exercises more ramified and subtle control. From block to block, as I looked and listened to the sounds around me, I found myself more sensually part of the whole energy. By that time there was no going back: no way of forgetting the situation. Only passivity had made it possible, as though I had temporarily become just what Condillac used to call man: a bundle of sense organs. Environing sense-impressions wrapped me on Sophocles Street.

Fortunately, though, Greece has a god for these moments. In the moment of feeling them Dionysus seems to give himself back as life. When he does, he dignifies the sensuous moment with a strange transcendence. It takes a degree of imagination, I suppose, to recognize the god here. But he gives signs. On Sophocles Street his sign is grain, just as it was in the shadowy early Greek centuries. This harvested grain lying around in sacks is part of the mystic, fertile body of the god himself, living in the spirit of the crops, once more to be eaten by his devotees, until he rearises in their strengthened bodies, his spring. I thought of this and felt less alone in the furious, dusty street. Dionysus was here too.

I found the other familiar street markets in Athens, on Hermes Street or on Aeolus and Athena Streets, in the lively cramped area under the shadow, and to the northeast, of the Acropolis. I had forgotten their schedules. Many of these markets were now held only

on occasional, appointed days, and were a less formal or rooted part
of the city than the Sophocles Street market. My first rediscovery of
the Athena market, though, was a revelation. I had forgotten that
it is only a fruit market. Carts of fruit were wheeled alongside the
curbs and sold to the housewives of the city. Confusion and energy
were added by the business in the regular shops which continued to
function as though no new market were active directly in front of
them.

The chief force I gathered from the fruit market was its brilliance. Melons, oranges, lemons, bananas were piled onto the light
carts like rind-bound concentrations of sunlight. Each pile seemed
to glow out from a luminous centre. Hawking these objects, by perfect contrast, stood black-dressed, austere peasant women or their
black-suited husbands. Most of these people had evidently come in
from outlying villages for the day. Truck gardening, I gather, is
still mainly unmechanized in Greece. Fruits and vegetables were
brought into the city on donkey carts, which entered early, and in
great interweaving lines, along the roads northwest to Eleusis, or
south to Sunium. Late in the night they would leave, moving stilly
back to the still land. The melons stayed on the tables of Athenian
ladies, and spoke even to their high-heeled guests of the potent,
authentic earth.

There were also the Athenian meat markets, which I punished
myself into revisiting. Cows (relatively few), sheep, rabbits, and
God knows what else were draining, hung openly from hooks
through the feet. Flies moved thickly over the flesh, while private
butchers negotiated with the market managers for the best cuts.
Cats prowled in the corners of the sheds, making occasional forays
toward or through the pools of blood, while the hanging animals,
head down, stared at the world out of empty, moodless eye sockets.

Such markets are no place for the sentimentalist, of whom there are few in Greece. Greeks have no society for the prevention of cruelty to animals. (I remember once trying to find shelter for a cat in Salonika.) Yet there is some consolation, even for the soft hearted, in these scenes; you need only reconcile yourself to the fact of man's animal nature and of his need to destroy in order to live. I tried to think this through. It was the consolation of encountering this destruction in an open, unfancied form, in which the slaughter of the innocents did not dress itself seductively. Here, at least, there was no hiding man's fundamental life-giving and death-giving transaction with nature.

Even in the Athenian meat market, Dionysus was still living. In that, as in the other open markets of the city, a deep closeness of nature to humanity was present. These markets, I thought, were so many life lines by which the only partially urbanized Athenian could reach back toward the natural cosmos which was the source of his power.

Man can go back to nature in a thousand ways, but none seems to give him more new life than the return to the sea. Bathing is only a mild taste of this immersion, this natural baptism. Bathing, a man governs the pond of water into which he lowers his flesh. He maintains a control. But the sea governs us, tempting us with its power, which is so vast, which yet allows us to use it gracefully, in a temporary self-aggrandizement. These thoughts Athens gave me that year.

Every large city, I concluded, should have a sea near it as a reminder of one of the four elemental forces of our world. Athens has the Aegean at its doorstep, beside the Piraeus. The Piraeus itself is not simply an annex of Athens, or a mere port. It is an independent and rapidly growing commercial city. Yet from Athens,

Piraeus seems a suburb, a dependency: the eyes reinforce this impression as they see the long active port spread at the foot of the Attic plain, "down-under" hill-crowned Athens.

The Athenians—and I with them—seemed to travel daily, and in number, down the plain to that sea. (They would also go east, to the other coast of Attica, to the simpler enticement of fishing villages like Porto Rafina.) The west coast of Attica was lined with beaches, stretching from Piraeus all the way to Sunium. Those around Piraeus were the least pristine, the most commercialized. Some had fences cast around them and had been converted into municipal beaches. To these, it seemed to me, the mass of Athenian swimmers went: the busses would stop obligingly, by prearrangement, at the municipal beaches, while only automobile owners could travel easily down the coast to farther, Edenic beach spots: to Varkisa or to Vouliagmene.

It was my observation that the Athenians go to the beach to find themselves in nature again, ultimately to worship in that experience which I have been calling Dionysus. Yet the Athenian does not enter the water as a native element. Vigorous, manly combat with the waves, the oceanic spirit, is rarely seen on these coasts. It is reserved for the Nordic or the Oriental swimmer. The Athenian seems to return to the autumn sea warily, even suspiciously. In this wariness, I imagine, the contemporary Greek shows his kinship with ancient Greek mariners, who, though skilled on, and used to, the water, always sailed close to shore, because they dreaded an entire horizon full of sea. That was too much. That was ocean.

Near the sea the Athenians talked more than usually—thus a lot —laughed a great deal, took off more clothes than usual. At first I was surprised, even though I'd seen it before. I should have been better prepared. It was, after all, chiefly in the sombre north or in New England that the sea has inspired gloomy meditation or a

sense of human finitude. The Aegean acts differently on men. It is
a finite sea: tideless, translucent, strictly defined by its coasts. And
it is beautiful, with an exciting repertoire of colors which centres
on turquoise as norm, and wavers frequently toward its opposed
extremes of black or pale blue. Athenians seemed to become inwardly illuminated in the presence of all this.

The removal of clothes was, I concluded, one sign of their joy.
Civilization is a pretense—though in the service of the highest human tradition—and it makes a fetish, as well as a convenience, of
clothing. In the great civilized centres of the world adequate bodily
clothing is required. Such modesty compels in London, Caracas, and
Tokyo: it is integral to the civilized endeavor, and has roots, I
think, in the collective wish to conceal and control the organs of
reproduction, those unruly and undiscriminating means to propaga-
tion. But by the sea, out of the immediate magnetic field of society,
close to the intensely present force of external nature, the urge to
exist in nature's way is strong. Undressing then seems a way of un-
covering the true self. (Though psychiatry acquaints us with other
motives mixed into that act: "indecent" components, which have
tainted us only through our long hibernation in a too proper
society.)

The Athenians went down to the sea in few clothes, as few as
permitted by the posted sign, which read, "Swimming in under-
pants prohibited." The average swimmer—I speak like a sociolo-
gist now—was likely to purchase his lunch at the beach pavilion;
he would collect an omelette, some salad, some retsina, and take it
back with him to the sand for consumption. There small groups—
more sociology—would form: a family, lovers, students of the
same sex. High-mooded, gay conversation would move out over the
sea. The waves taking it all in silently.

Those same people were not good swimmers, on the average.

This held especially for the city dwellers. I mean here something different from their wariness about the water: I mean their heaviness *in* the water. As a people the Greeks—those of today—are unathletic. (How athletic can a man with a moustache be?) They seemed to swim by preference on their backs (like me), or surrounded by jocular rubber horses. Families would paddle about together. People of all ages smiled and squealed: bourgeois rebaptism.

Occasionally something luminous happened, and I saw the meaning of this large-scale trek to the municipal beaches. I resort to a single example. In a moment of wonderful indolence I was lying stretched out, reading *Vanity Fair,* on the Phaleron beach. I swim badly and was tired from the little I had done. A girl was lying alone, in the middle of the beach. There were perhaps ten other people around, most of them middle-aged, talking, resting. The sun was low and the sky perfectly clear, signed with that kind of finality which often marks the end of a Mediterranean day. Out of the shower house behind me came three young men in their bathing suits, walking toward the restaurant. When they came to the girl, who was lying flat on her stomach, apparently resting, they stopped and looked. I looked at her too, then, and saw how unusual she was. She had dark-olive flesh and black hair, which hung rather droopingly over her shoulders. Her back was toward me: it was firm, delicately trenched around its backbone. Her legs were thin and long. There was a kind of glisten to her whole body from a half-dried film of water, seen now in the luminous, lowering air.

As I watched, one of the men leaned over and touched her damp hair, then put his hand on her neck. It was bare—she was wearing a short two-piece bathing suit. She shook the hand away with a sudden motion of her rising head. It was not quite clear how the gentle touch was meant, or how she interpreted it. There was something almost ritualistic in the movements. The man squatted and stroked her again, this time touching her low on the back. This time there was no doubt. The other two men muttered something low and smiled at each other. One of them touched her foot with his foot. By this time she was sitting up straight: she had a neat, hard body; her black eyes were outraged as she looked at the men. It was no prudish look—she seemed an experienced girl, somehow. Rather, she appeared to say that she found this behavior salacious and base. The men had expected her to like it, but when she faced them they stepped back. Even they reserved themselves before her. The fact that, in standing straight before them, she showed them a beautiful, young body even less covered than they had supposed at first, showing her hip bones and her long tan thighs, was no incentive to their desire. She made them transcend themselves.

In that instant she turned and raced into the sea, as lightly and rapidly as music. The men stood watching—as did the others on the beach—while she threw herself into the now gray-blue, totally placid water and swam fast out into it. She moved swiftly, cleaving the water with the least possible disturbance. We could see her head go up and down and her legs move organically; we felt her stillness, isolation, and wholeness in that sea. I think she assumed, in that instant, a kind of symbolic force for the group on the beach. Even those men seemed to know it. Her motion carried all of our senses of return deeply in its wake and left the incident of the hands to oblivion. She was with the true Dionysus now.

"Sympathy" is a fundamental form of group infection, in which an emotion communicates itself electrically among the members of a group. Common hate, common desire, common fear—any of these may be contents of this spreading mood. It is not easy to check, and it may be dangerously uncontrollable. There is a semi-

physical infection which is comparable to this psychic one. I am not
thinking of disease, which strikes its victim in his passivity, "un-
selving" him, so to speak. I mean, here, the mere excited awareness
of your own physical continuity with other bodies. This may or may
not be a sexual awareness. Frequently it is not. On Athenian busses
it probably is. I rode them enough to find out.

The typical Athenian bus was still an ancient import from America, creaky in the gears, half painted, noisy above the usual noises
of the city's traffic. It had two managers: a driver and a ticket seller,
who moved painstakingly through the crowd. These two men
would remain in perfect communion—frequently mystic—with
one another, although they were often separated by a moving wall
of passengers. The driver never left a stop before he had received
some signal from his mate. Sometimes a bell would give the signal,
sometimes not. Perhaps sometimes the men communicated like in-
sects, with humanly inaudible sounds.

Sometimes there were fifty or sixty passengers between driver
and conductor. Such an overcrowded bus seems to be a familiar
phenomenon in all cities of the world. It is part of the increasingly
acute traffic problem which threatens to suffocate cities. But the
situation in Greece—or, rather, in the Mediterranean—is special.
There the overcrowding of busses arises from more than necessity;
it is not simply that a great many people must travel simultaneously
in the same direction. Up to a certain point, and varying with the
case, these people enjoy their crowded rides. I became convinced of
this. They enjoy a sense of bodily continuity.

I came to know this from faces, from ways of talking, and from
less conspicuous signs. I knew it from a certain *Gestalt* of feeling
which pervaded most of the urban busses. It would be a feeling of
happy physical oneness: was this sexual? Largely yes. But not evil.
Highly spiritual ceremonies have grown from just this kind of

sense of oneness: the *orgai* of early Greece are an instance. Spirituality has often grown from sexuality. A diffuse sexual infection was strong on the Athenian busses.

Yet such infection was not the only aspect of bodily communion. There would always be a sense of camaraderie, expressed in shouts back and forth, in random political conversations, in jokes with the conductor. Snatches of music would be heard: a boy would sing. The driver would go careening through the twilight, turning to talk to a man behind him or crossing himself as he passed a church. Before him would be flowers set in a thin vase, and an icon. The bus strangely homelike, uniquely homelike.

The desire for togetherness has taken unexpected forms. In one easy-to-parody American incarnation, togetherness becomes a saccharine family closeness. In Communist Russia the spirit of togetherness takes—reputedly—the form of a sense of social oneness, of disinclination to privacy. In Mediterranean countries togetherness often has a public direction, as in the ideal Communist state. But in Greece, so far as I can see it, this public direction usually has no political or "organizational" ingredient. In politics, every Greek is private, infinitely individual. Mediterranean togetherness springs from a sense of the oneness of human beings, bodily or spiritual, sexual or religious.

Group intuition of this oneness is, I believe, a way of thinking back through the blood to stages of less biological differentiation among human beings, when we all more closely resembled our mutual ancestors. Under the new uniformities which society proposes, and the new individualities which we adopt in order to distinguish ourselves, there remains the old uniformity of the first days of the human adventure. Dionysus is there when we come through our feelings onto that uniformity. Hence the deep emotion associated with membership in a crowd. Hence the strange universality of a ride in a crowded Athenian bus.

The Athenian Acropolis is sanctified still today by some abiding presence of Athena, the virgin goddess sprung from Zeus' forehead and the patroness of wisdom. I speak metaphorically, but somehow, I think, in the language of experience. To that language it is no secret that Athena usually wages tacit warfare with Dionysus: she standing for all he overthrows. Her devotees—like Pentheus in Euripides' *Bacchae*—have given their lives to her cause, the cause of rational order. Creon himself, in *Antigone,* is one of her faithful. Others there are, even gods, who are unable to understand her adequately. Apollo, in Aeschylus' *Oresteia,* has sanctioned Orestes' slaying of his mother, but Athena, true to her nature, countermands the divine intervention on behalf of vendetta killing. She saves Orestes, but only on condition that he be part of a new order of justice. That trilogy ends with the victory of Athena over Apollo, and with the consequent foundation of a law court (the Areopagus) in Athens. Rationality, as the principle of civilization, triumphs.

The closeness of ancient Athens to Athena, its patron goddess, is of inestimable significance. This is not simply a literary point. The whole bond between civilization and reason or order is implied in this closeness. Yet historians of Greek religion have qualifications to write into the notion that Athena was the dominant goddess of the Athenians. Especially since the study of folklore and nature myth has taken the field, there has been mounting interest in the complex structure of ancient religious experience. Jane Ellen Harrison, in *Themis,* examined the nature cults and hero cults of Greece, bringing startling evidence of the importance of non-Olympic deities in ancient Greece. Among these usually less-than-respectable cults which coexisted with the Olympic pantheon, and frequently flourished most verdantly in the popular mind, those of Orpheus and Pythagoras were typical. Most powerful was the cult of Dionysus.

I have said, already, that Dionysus was a complex god of passion, frivolity, and simple intoxication. These are the moods in which he appeared, took on existence. The moods in which he occurred to me, at least, during this Athenian stay. I speak of the matter this way because to the ancient Greeks, as I understand it, the existence of a god was the experience of him. The passionate mood in which Dionysus appeared was a directional experience: pointing toward procreation, the making of new vitality through one's own vitality. Athena, on the other hand, lived in those experiences which rendered the clarity, definiteness, and intelligibility of reality. Just as she herself was born from a forehead, pure intelligence without mother, so she is reborn in essentially virgin experience, the experience of form and reason. Form and reason are, in the roughest sense, ungenerative, static. They share the quietude of Plato's "forms" or "ideas" of things.

Dionysus and Athena complement one another, and between themselves exhaust the possibilities of our experience, as it can be considered under the aspects of reason and passion. All of this proved itself to me in every encounter with the Acropolis. And it served as a cautioning prelude to those encounters. For that great mesa of praise to Athena—the Parthenon being the virgin's own and the Nike temple a precious gift to her—seemed to me more than ever to invite a superficial understanding. All is so brilliantly gleaming there. The marble seems released out of its inner solitude into outer ecstasy by the all-eliciting sun. The world of things, especially the city and the hills, spreads around in all its surface excitement. On the Acropolis itself this brilliance is offered under the control of a—paradoxically—almost dizzying balance. The Parthenon's famous symmetry seems to seize the eye with all the contentless persuasion of a perfect geometric proof. Form and substance seem united to offer a mathematical demonstration of the beauty of the Acropolis. All this is Athena's work, which remains superficial unless experienced with Dionysus' help.

This danger is great because, no matter what spiritual equipment you bring to the Acropolis, you will find it hard to encounter Dionysus there during the day. In the sea or on a bus it is easier, but in the blaze of sun, at the top of the city, that god is reticent. He prefers night and the dark spirits running through the sinuous vine-root. But he is also on the Acropolis from dawn to sunset, staying there in harmony, almost in twinship, with Athena. His voice is lower than hers there, but only the meeting of their two voices composes the richest tone of the place. For the substantive passion in our experience of the Acropolis is Dionysus. He is that inner ecstasy which is lured by the sun into outer ecstasy. The control he longs for, and suffers under, is outer ecstasy, form and reason, Athena. He is the persuasion of deep, substantive feeling, she of mathematics.

Seldom is Dionysus, in fact, so fortunate as to find an adequate mating with the virgin goddess, a mating which permits the virgin to retain her virginity. Seldom is his procreative power so adequately received and contained as by the queen of the Acropolis. Seldom, in fact, is that Dionysus whom the Athenians so persistently, and often unknowingly, worship, as significant or beautiful as he is on the Acropolis. In the *taverna,* the mind of the language-maker, the sea, the bus, Dionysus comes fleetingly and transportingly, as violent as wine. On the Acropolis he sings in form.

Launched Again: Aegean Hopping

PART OF THE PROBLEM was how to divide my time. Sometime in late January I began to itch. There was a profusion of buds in a small garden where I often went to sit. I could see them working themselves out toward flowerhood. In the afternoon it would drizzle, every few days anyhow, and without quite realizing, I realized this meant the opening of a spring. From the Acropolis I could see the ocean moving, and I understood that something was beginning to move in me too.

With considerable sentiment I packed. By now my own feelings (and interests) had just begun to engage tightly with Athens again. Against the grain of them, I said good-bye to friends, bought tickets, and put out like a (very timid) ancient mariner onto a sea which I loved. I would not see Athens again this year.

I sailed onto that water which was beginning to move and beckon.

The island of Aegina lay an hour and a half by boat from Piraeus, but I had not yet been there this year. It would be the best place to start for the islands.

Aegina's short temporal distance from Athens was long enough for a great difference in atmosphere. Aegina was, as I remembered, always a good introduction to the Aegean Islands, all of which have moods, or beings, which completely distinguish them from the mainland. And which, unaccountably, unite them to one another in spirit.

Aegina was not the most distinctive of those islands: that was part of its interest. It did stand apart, though, and to some extent simply because of the significance and beauty of its ruins. I remembered the Temple of Aphaia, on the east coast of the island, as one of the purest remains of Greek architecture. The marble was fresh and active. Going over on the boat, it came to me how, on my first weekend in Greece, years before, I had climbed the hill from a small, blue-green Aeginetan harbor, and how the temple had appeared only gradually, in glimpses, among the thick trees above; how it was still enclosed in a grove, sacredly, as it had always been. How I had sworn love to Greece then.

This time, though, I headed for the town, taking a bus from the opposite coast. The trip was an introduction to Greek island hinterland. I watched it as though I had not seen it before. Everywhere were high, climbing hills; nowhere mountains. The soil was rocky and, that year, lavender with heather. A yellowish tint of marjoram. The land *seemed* utterly dry, as though it could support only its desiccated-looking, though thirst-quenching, crops; its vines and olive trees. The silver-gray flashes of olive leaves, against clear sky, represented everything pure and austere in the trip.

The villages through which the bus was passing were poor and forgotten. Low white houses, rutted streets, farm animals in the yards: here and there old women in black dresses and shawls. Life close to the Greek island soil imposed a distinctive style of life and architecture.

But in the town of Aegina, set like a metropolis in the plain on the west coast, many houses had two stories, the streets were broader, there was a domed metropolitan church, and, above all, there was great activity. The peak of activity was centred on the harbor.

It was immediately evident that Aegina was living from the sea, from a few tourists, and from a characteristic, coarse pottery which —I am told—has been made on that island since antiquity. (That "antiquity" which was never antiquity, but is only that to us.) The Aeginetans were manoeuvring around in small caïques, bringing back catches of *barbounia* and squid, or fat porous sponges. The harbor was crowded with boats and motion, all insheltered by the arms of the mole, which extended like an embrace from the town. At the end of one arm stood a small, whitewashed church, spiritual sentinel for the town. Walking along the road beside the water, and looking out to sea, I repeatedly found myself caught up in fish nets or tripping over clumps of drying squid.

Farther up the shore caïques were preparing to cross to another island. Their hulls were blue, orange, or green with inevitable names of girl friends or saints carelessly lettered across the prows. I wondered where they were going. Perhaps taking peasants off to a holiday with relatives. The passengers—I suppose—may have been interisland merchants. Goods were still transported that way. Eggs, chickens, and jugs of wine were handed from one passenger to another until a place was found for them. I watched the performance. Finally everything would be ready. The owner of the boat would be about to start the motor. Then he would pause, and come forward from the stern to see if more passengers were coming. Invariably an old woman in black would appear running from the other side of the street, holding three chickens by their feet, and calling to the owner to wait "in the name of the Virgin." While at the same time, the passengers were getting restless. Some demanded immediate departure. Some of them wanted to have the chickens or other livestock taken away from the interior of the caïque. Finally they sailed off.

In that confusion my instinct was to go eat. I thought at least that would be simple. The mere walking around on that island could be strenuous. And it wasn't just the noise and the contention. The colors were almost too strong and well defined. The sky was authentically blue: cloudless, outspread by a generous Titianesque Zeus; surrounding a sun which was still and purifying. The whiteness of the harbor-lining houses glistened, opening forth from surfaces, assailing my eye demandingly, unremittingly. Then there were the other senses. I could smell the water, the fish (of course), and the bending oleanders in a weird, active synthesis. I was starved.

But the competition for eating was strong. Around the harbor the restaurant tables were outside, often extending across the sidewalk in front of the establishment, sometimes even out into the perilous street. The waiters were circulating at a dogtrot among the widespread metal tables. The chairs were full, if not with diners— which is likely in a country of endless dinner conversations—then with newspaper readers and coffee drinkers. I had to break into the tight network.

Once I found a table the struggle was over. The course of energies flowed about and around, not against. The waiters brushed by me in their haste. Volatile conversation hemmed in my table from all sides. The food came promptly. For the first time since I arrived, the surrounding harbor scene began to take place around a centre, me. It was no longer a question simply of moving with the day and its brilliance. Now I could watch. It was easier. I chewed

squid, drank resinated wine, and listened to the stillness of two hundred agitated voices.

I suppose I should have stayed. A few days should have become a month, should have become a quarter of a year. It was impossible. Something told me to make a geographical whole. I pushed toward Syra. The weather was perfect for the sea. Sitting, sitting, feeling.

Every Aegean boat trip is powerful. It seeps into the texture of experience, resurges continuously in memory. The more so, because of the similarity of all such trips.

First there is a potent natural sense-environment. Bright, pellucid sea, azure sky, a clear, blowing air's increasing velocity. Your skin grows salty and damp. The other passengers on deck are probably quite indifferent to one another, caught up in the newness of their own almost forgotten sense-existences. Some, probably the Greeks in the crowd, may be bent under deck umbrellas or in the shelter of cabins. A few scarved and long-haired foreigners (like me) will be found striding the deck, watching the bubbling foam churned up like seablood by the keel.

There is also the music which, to my ears, lends savor to the trip. (I have no delicate ear.) It will be spread by loud-speaker from a phonograph lodged in the lounge. The selections are harsh and noisy versions of the top Greek popular songs of the day—almost of the hour, there as here. The alchemy is this: the mood of the alternately sentimental or virile pieces blends with the blowing air, and with the energy of the sea-cleaving ship, to loosen you. Massiness, the inert world of body, seems to have been transmuted. Islands start to slip by like thoughts and to vanish beyond the ship's movement. Time falls away from consciousness, too, as the endless music picks itself up for indefinite repetition.

Nothing, in fact, gave me the old Greek feelings more, that

year, than the ride from Aegina to Syra. I forget the stages of emotion now, but I remember clearly, at least, that at sunset the mood began to change. It was still three hours to Syra. A number of islands had been passed, some close, their details visible. (The Aegean is an intimate sea.) In the clear sunset the islands were lying passively on the water, were buoyant looking against the darkening sky. They were weightless. Gradually their humping spines were drawn down into night, while the last luminous glances of sun retracted into their Great Eye. Stars had begun to shine even before the sun was extinguished, and the moon had begun to mount a totally open sky, defining the indefinible, rewakening mythic vision of a moon goddess ascending the sky in her chariot. I was just beginning to sense how the Aegean people were able to shape their myths, inherited from a more passionate and extravagant East, into uniquely disciplined aesthetic awareness.

Night came on, dinners were served, the lounges filled. The air grew damper on deck, but was still soft, a blithe (though blown) presence. I was hoping for the luck of seeing Syra when it first appeared; though I remembered what luck that involved; that you should just happen to look up from a conversation to see, scattered close together in the descended night, a dense miraculous constellation of lights. I remember how the lights would seem, at first, to be on the sea. The sea would seem to be rising into the sky. The town of Syra is hilly. Its lights appear on houses around the hills. Seen in the night the lights look removed from support, accidents deprived of substance.

I missed the beginning of the miracle this time. Someone touched my arm, and pointed. I saw then. But there were good moments coming. As we approached, the scene began to change character. The water and night were still in a blackness so thick that the boat seemed static in the stiff, dense atmosphere. But the lights on Syra were changing. Now I saw many of them for signs. Most of them were advertising, in tall, garish, pallor-diffusing letters, the chief commodity of the island; Turkish delight, *loukoumi*. Some of the signs were yellow, others red, others blue: the lights were fierce and hypnotic. The long, anticipant waterfront spread below them, while people gathered gradually to watch the boat glide in from the night like a dream, or like that idyll boat that once took Odysseus back from Phaeacia to his own Ithaca. Behind the signs and the harbor the town lights were glistening, now like stars, and following their respective streets in receding lines, pausing only occasionally to surround an elongated piazza.

Everything, of course, was entirely different when we had disembarked. Syra is a mid-point on most trips through the Aegean: the passenger ships usually stop there in the evening, long before their passengers are ready for sleep, but yet, somehow, close to the end of the day. For such people, I suppose, the going forth for an hour on Syra at those times takes place in a dreamlike mood. The people on the quais, the bright, nearly empty restaurants blaring music, and the quiet back streets probing into the town: all this is there, before you, but somehow, also, only in you.

The mood of the approach to Syra was, and is, also dreamlike. But, as I felt this time, the unreality of Syra itself was harder to explain. It became clear to my feeling, this time, only when I had penetrated into the town, down one of the long side streets. Suddenly, perhaps in the course of a single block, the uncanny blackness and silence of the area made itself felt. Then there was a square, and on it numbers of people walking slowly and peacefully, back and forth, in the leisure of aristocrats. Hand in hand, arm in arm, they were strolling. The talk was low, there were few sounds, and a thin breeze was faintly audible in the pepper trees as I joined the walkers in the square for a while. It was like a disembodied parade, this walk. Here, precisely, the image of Homer's Phaeacians returned to me. These Syrans seemed to be Phaeacians—contented, aristocratic aesthetes, lost in the misty sea. Syra was Phaeacia.

Leaving the walkers I wandered aimlessly in the back streets of the town, where the darkness became denser. Now there were few people. The houses were prosperous but silent: their two-storied façades, with grillwork balconies and wide doors, watched impassively. The streets were broad but empty. Small-bulbed street lights, which had been visible from the harbor, worked only half-effectually to hold back the blackness. I found myself, not realizing it fully at first, turning back toward the bright water front.

In the boat again, as it began to leave, and the wind grew, the Homeric thought came back. Even the *loukoumi* signs helped. They added a brash piquancy which gave the scene character, just as the music on board had heightened the afternoon in the sun. With increase in distance the island turned more uncompromisingly into dream. Most of the passengers had gone down to their hot cabins now. As the *loukoumi* lights withered away from the wound-healing black night, there remained the most intense memory of all: the quiet, handsome, slow-moving walkers in the lost square of Syra.

Tinos, no less than Syra, requires simply to be met under the right circumstances. It is possible to visit the island without feeling its distinctness. (I had done so once.) The town of Tinos itself, on the south coast, is a characteristic Greek island village. Its stucco houses are perhaps unusually shiny: their whiteness is intense under noon sun. The greenery in the town, set off against the restless water of the harbor, asks much of your visual energy. The whole settlement is topped, at the end of its long, main avenue, by a white cathedral and monastery. Yet even in those details there is nothing uncharacteristic of a Greek island town.

That day I walked some miles down the coast, at the advice of the *Guide Bleu,* to the ruins of the Temple of Poseidon. The day was translucid, all natural objects seeming to be divested of their surfaces—barks, skins, stones falling away to leave lightness and the airy centre of being. Even the ruins—foundations of the temple and of a refectory—were translated that day. Little was left there, but much could be felt. The spirit of Poseidon was near, breathed out, it seemed to me, by the muttering, almost still bay beside the ruins. Like so many Greek architectural offerings to gods, this temple was placed in physical proximity to the god's nature. The rudimentary but clear and formed stones of the foundations were as whole as the sea.

Yet all this, it seemed then and seems now, looking back, did not distinguish Tinos fundamentally from other Aegean islands. Each was a sensuous experience of great intensity and complexity. Each had some meaningful nook of ruins, and removed beaches. The uniqueness of Tinos, as I half suspected, lay in another direction.

Tinos is the most important cult and pilgrimage centre in the Aegean. In 1881 a miracle-working icon was found on the island: a sign, ostensibly, of the Virgin's particular favor. At that time the cathedral was constructed at the summit of the town, to house the potent icon. The cathedral and its monastery were to become, through subsequent reputation as a healing spot, the Lourdes or Ste. Anne de Beaupré of the Aegean. Twice a year pilgrimages of thirty to forty thousand believers make their ways to Tinos. Many of these people are ill or crippled, and hope to be cured. Many—no doubt the majority—want simply to worship, harboring the thought that the Virgin may address them. The nave of the church is crowded with the rich ex-votos left by satisfied believers.

This "fact" about Tinos may remain inert, or become immensely alive in experience. I caught the aliveness this time through participation in the pilgrimage. I happened onto the event by luck, stepping unsuspectingly into that maelstrom of worshippers. I was swallowed by movement.

The notion of stepping into a river fits. In full noon, I remembered, Tinos is still and placid. But on pilgrimage nights the town is transmuted. This night, all its whiteness was still white, the water was still soughing and stirring in the harbor. But on every side bodies were moving, strenuously, hopingly, if not rapidly. It was like the body of some single, vast animal. The river was their sweeping, inexorable drive toward the cathedral.

Before the pilgrims, that night, stretched the brightly illuminated, hill-mounting main street of Tinos, with the far brighter cathedral at its summit. The whole length of that cobblestoned street swarmed with ascending people, many, as was clear even at a distance, moving their crippled or sick bodies with difficulty. It was a scene from the *Purgatorio*. Above hung a warm, black sky. There was great tension and directed effort in the world.

As I began to climb with the group, its inner impulsion was transmitted. The always uncomfortable situation of being a mere spectator of what others believe could be partially overcome here. Physical participation drew us all together—on one level—with elementary, transcendent force. The walking was hard: continually blocked ahead or hindered behind by the irregular, worn cobblestones.

The steeper slopes of the hill were lined with booths where "religious" items were on sale. On the bright, makeshift shelves lay all kinds of long, beeswax candles, garish icons, and prayer beads. The nearer we came to the sanctum itself, the larger and more elaborately stocked were the booths.

Climbing, I grew simultaneously more aware of two distinct features in the scene: of the physical misery of many of the climbers;

and of the strange, rather insubstantially radiant façade of the cathedral. Many of the climbers were old. Some were clearly *mutilés de la guerre;* others were badly diseased. A few were carried on makeshift stretchers. There were also some families: they were the main centres of exuberance. Yet a kind of joy pervaded the whole undertaking, the joy of hope.

Above this striving and hoping, the cathedral glistened like a promised land (or a huge wedding cake). It was white, illuminated by bright bulbs. That radiance, I thought, would be visible far out to sea. Around the neo-Byzantine façade, with its bright cupolas, ran the walls of a surrounding monastery. They too shone in the night; a dormitory for angels. But there was something thin about the vision, as if it might be just about to vanish. Almost as though, even in that setting of human misery, we were simply at a play.

The illusion was partially dispelled by the courtyard at the top of the hill, immediately before the cathedral. There hundreds of pilgrims lay on the stones. Many were sleeping, covered with thin blankets, and curled, when possible, against the walls of the surrounding monastery. The less fortunate were nearer the centre of the square, nearer the feet of the just arriving pilgrims as they made their way to the church. Tinos is a small town, and there were few accommodations: the sleepers and the sufferers did their best to solve the housing problem, and spread themselves out in the night like pious corpses.

The waves of climbers passed them, and entered the church. Outside it was night, inside full day, as the worshippers took places body to body to watch the continuous service. All was gold and silver inside: silver-framed icons, silver offerings in the form of ships hung from the ceiling, the altar and the iconostasis gleaming with valuable stones. All this bathed in the enriching, waxy light of candles—those held by pilgrims, and those situated around the nave.

The light had a fluidity of its own, deeper and more magical than sunlight.

Having come so far, I felt nearly impelled into belief. The others moved forward to communion, to place adoring lips on jewelled icons, to kneel before revered objects and people. The uncompromising fullness of the instant held the church in tension, while incessant, disciplined chanting confirmed the moment of joy. Then the worshippers passed to smaller sanctuaries, eventually to leave, to return onto themselves in the other world, our world. A new group entered. More surged up the hill behind them.

Chios abounds in both nature and history. That large island, some five miles off the coast of Asia Minor, is a complex experience, and though my direction was Crete, before Asia Minor, I took advantage of boat schedules to make Christian Chios the continuation of Christian Tinos.

In contrast to many Aegean islands, Chios is fertile. Vegetables and fruit are raised in quantity there, and an aromatic gum, *mastika*, popular for chewing and distilling into a liqueur of the same name. Cotton, almonds, and olives are cultivated. In all this, the island resembles juicy neighbors, like Mytilene or Samos, or even the rich Asia Minor coast.

The town of Chios itself is the main centre of the island. There, it seemed to me, I touched historical richness at every turn. In an old mosque there was a museum, with a collection of ancient pottery, reminding of the long, significant pre-Christian history of the island. Next to the port was the huge *Kastro*, a walled-in, once-armed fortification which was first built in the ninth century, and successively used by Venetians, Genoese, Franks, Catalans, and Turks—until final expulsion of the last named, during the Greek War of Independence. The modern town, by contrast, seemed to

me very much of our century, with considerable commercial activity, automobiles, and bright lights. It lacks depth.

The *Kastro* has remained one of the most impressive forms of Chiote history today. In those walls lies the so-called Turkish quarter, an area preserving Turkish houses, Turkish dress—in short a "romantically" Turkish atmosphere—as well as any part of the Greek world. (This is by no means, I think, the atmosphere of present-day Istanbul or Ankara; rather of French romantic paintings of the Levant, of works by Delacroix or Ingres. It is *absolutely not* the atmosphere of Turkish Cyprus.) The denizens of the Chios *Kastro* are predominantly Greek with some Turkish blood in the veins.

I found the *Kastro* impressive just because it did fulfill some of those stock romantic expectations which our time seldom satisfies. I walked through the *Kastro* on narrow, curving streets, over cobblestones, under jutting balconies. Archways led off into dark courtyards. Still narrower side routes branched off into alleys with small, gray façades. Something gave the inhabitants of the area an air of mystery, unclarity, unpredictability. Old women sat on their balconies smoking thin cigars. It was this slightly ominous air of mystery which seemed to me to distinguish the Chios *Kastro* from, say, the *Altstadt* at Tübingen, the *vieille ville* at Périgueux, or the *vecchia città* at Bari. I encountered, here, a difference between the spirits of pastness in Western Europe and in the Near East.

The Byzantine past, the historical groundwork for Turkish influence throughout Greece, enjoys distinguished presence on Chios. One of the finest Byzantine churches of Greece, Nea Mone, is two and a half hours (by bus, then mule) inland from the town of Chios. Food, energy, and open eyes are prerequisites for the trip.

An hour and a half by mule from the bus terminus, a simple village, I caught sight of Nea Mone. It was among hills, well hidden in high trees, in the midst of a green landscape. The church itself was small, almost inconspicuous, with characteristic low, tiled cupolas, and a small courtyard. A few dormitory buildings remained from the time when Nea Mone was an important monastery. An old refectory was near them. But everything seemed to have fallen into placid desuetude now, only a guardian monk or two remaining. Caught in sun, buried in the mood of rich, surrounding foliage, the courtyard folded over onto itself in unconditional surrender to time.

The energy of the place was within, where, in the last years, art historians have been actively supervising the restoration of the Nea Mone mosaics in the nave and the apse of the church. Those mosaics are the chief fame of the church, and the core of its existence. Created in the eleventh century, they deal with events in the New Testament from the Annunciation to Pentecost. Well restored, these scenes live again out of the original, potent spirit of the man who made them.

By climbing scaffolds, and crouching in nooks, I was able to confront those works directly. Byzantine church mosaics demand this, having been created with strong, vertical immediacy, eminently facing you. In such a small church as Nea Mone, this demand is forceful. It is as ineluctable now as it can ever have been.

Christ, the three Marys, and the Roman centurion became the dramatis personae of the event of my presence in that church. The main characters of the gospel narrative appeared and reappeared over the walls, volatilizing themselves to spirit, acting again in my eyes the old story. Nothing was still in the nave. To the pure directness and motion of the mosaicked walls and ceilings potent color was added. Juxtaposed yellows and reds, blues and golds made these works as sense-awakening as any in the Byzantine tradition. Among them, I lost all sense of body.

It was in this transmutation of body into sense, of sense into re-fined, narrative-following feeling, that I became aware of the energy of Nea Mone. With this awareness came a second one, scarcely more than an intuition: how odd it seemed, there in that secluded, hard-to-reach cupola-covered building, under a usual summer sun, to be so beleaguered by this aesthetic demand, and by the religious force to which it had given form. Nea Mone is demanding, and giving, like Chios itself.

Crete: Deeply South

IN MANY WAYS Crete is the most romantic part of the Greek world. The simple thought of it had drawn me, in those years of absence from Greece, as much as any of my Hellenic memories. I remembered how my senses, even the unity of my entire sense-life, had been stimulated there.

The sensuousness of Crete, I think, was evident already in the myths through which most of us have made our first acquaintance with the island—the myths of Minos, Phaedra, Icarus, and Ariadne. Often Greek myths are too complex and too subtle in implication to be met romantically, in fullness of feeling. When I think of the exploits of Heracles, of the Argonauts, or of the experience of Oedipus, I find myself involved either with ambiguities and implications or with the intellectual-narrative interest of the theme. Such stories don't speak to my blood. The main myths of Crete, in my case anyway, offer themselves with a strange openness to the emotions. I *feel* my ways into them.

At its strongest, I believe, the emotion-addressing power of Cretan myths is primitive, takes us back toward Hittite and Sumerian tradition, toward that ancient Near East with which early Crete had strong ties. The story of Minos, Pasiphae, and the Minotaur is a product of an early civilization's psychology, though admittedly such psychology speaks clearly to us too. (How advanced is *our* culture, after all?)

Minos was the legendary ruler of Crete, sharing the kingdom with his brothers, and reproducing bountifully with his wife Pasiphae. Then he wished to have the rule to himself, and drove out his brothers, with Poseidon's help. Out of gratitude for this help, Minos asked Poseidon to send from the sea a fine bull, which he, Minos, could sacrifice to the god. The snow-white bull which was sent was so beautiful that Minos could not bear to kill it, and substituted another for it. At this substitution Poseidon grew furious. He brought trouble into the ruler's life.

Poseidon chose a revenge fitting with his brutal nature, the malign character for which Odysseus had known him, and by which Poseidon had, in distinction to Aphrodite of the placid sea, been known as the god of stormy and high-waved seas. Poseidon caused Pasiphae, Minos' wife, to fall desperately in love with the bull which Minos had spared; thus the god made destructive the very thing which Minos had considered too beautiful to kill. The irony in Poseidon's revenge is the cruelest trait of the myth. With Poseidon's help, Pasiphae was able to fulfill her passion for the bull, and to conceive the Minotaur in a labyrinth, built especially for it, and from that point, as is the habit with good ancient myths, the story ramifies out into several legends.

We learn of the yearly tribute of Athens to the Minotaur, and of the eventual success of the Athenian Theseus in killing the beast in the labyrinth. (The complications of Theseus' return with Ariadne, the King's daughter, whom he left on Naxos, then of Theseus' fateful home-coming at Athens, are well known, and initiate a new generation of tales.) We learn too of Daedalus, who had been the architect of the maze, and who was imprisoned in it, with his son Icarus, for having helped Theseus find his way into the centre of the labyrinth. From that centre, furthermore, Daedalus and Icarus made their famous flight, which took the father to Sicily, the son to a flaming death. These flights are themselves poetic bridges to new themes. There are various legends about the later wandering and cult of Daedalus. The imaginative creativity which first expressed itself in the story of Minos and Poseidon—if indeed that was a starting point and not simply a stage in a far older myth now lost— that imaginative creativity found itself almost indefinitely perpetuated. The Cretan story had such initial richness, that, like a fertile protozoon, it multiplied itself rapidly.

My main point is simply the emotional directness of the Cretan myth. At its centre it conveys a tone of bestial and introverted passion: Pasiphae and the bull recur to the feelings most, establishing themselves at the centre. Only in terms of their meaningful, consequential union does the conventional picture of Minos as a throne-usurper or a wise lawgiver become more than usually interesting. By Pasiphae's passion, Minos is drawn into an atmosphere of corruption, thus of moral implications. That same passion, with what it says about the darknesses of the body, casts a shadow over all the subsequent events of the myth. Theseus, Ariadne, Daedalus, Icarus, Phaedra: all are tainted—and heightened in "interest"—by their connection with a corrupt passion. This outspreading mood of corruption is not the same one that we find in, for example, the Oedipus legend. Incest had its distinctive horror in classical antiquity. Yet, even as it strikes Oedipus, it seems a scandal of fate, a dreadful misfortune to be understood, from the onus of which there may be —as in *Oedipus at Colonus*—eventual release. But there is nothing "understandable" about Pasiphae's passion. A cause is offered in the myth: Poseidon's anger. But the passion itself is left in the foreground, the object of chief interest. It is the passionate anti-intelligibility of the chief Cretan myth which impresses us. It is here that Crete's "romantic" openness to passionate feeling is most characteristically foreshadowed.

Coming into this world from the Aegean was strong stuff. I think I have gotten at something of the evanescence of the Aegean islands. They are—wonderfully—never quite real. Totally unlike them, the town of Heraklion, capital of Crete, confronted me really, firmly in the senses: it is distinctly more Southern in appearance than any place on the Greek mainland or islands, just as it is in the deep south geographically. In the Peloponnesus—say at Sparta or Kalamata—palm trees can be found. There is considerable greenery, relatively high rainfall. But there is more of both commodities in Heraklion. I noticed it instantly. In addition, the air was softer, not with the rather austere, purifying heat of the Greek mainland, but with what was more nearly a balmy warmth. The sky was soft and formed less immaculate outlines along the silhouetting world: trees, houses, monuments remained more closed in on their own beings, less incandescently opened outward. Heraklion was informal. The main street of the town was busy, lined with hotels, restaurants, stores, and offices of shipping agents. I saw good evidence of prosperity. The city was a successful entrepôt, receiving the agricultural products of much of the island for export, and receiving water-transported goods for distribution throughout the island. The bay was large and serviceable. I passed sailors and ship captains mingling with merchants. Yet the mood was of a small town. People appeared to know one another. Pedestrians, and farmers with sheep, crossed or walked down the street casually, as indifferent as possible to the occasional antiquated Ford taxis blasting horns behind them.

Certain of the walkers provided a visible introduction to the Southern Greekness of the island. I knew that the men of Crete were famous for their good looks and their courage. In the last war they fought the Germans bitterly from every mountain and copse of the island. Such *pallikaria*—one name for the Cretan mountain men —were in evidence even in Heraklion, the "big city" as far as they were concerned. They were dressed darkly, generally wearing black, baggy-kneed trousers—a Turkish style, originally, thanks to the long occupation of the island—trousers which fitted loosely into high boots. Their shirts were lighter, buttoned at the neck. Color entered with the bags slung over the men's shoulders. These wool bags were brilliant, of different pattern and color on their two sides, and used for every imaginable practical purpose—a true case of the meeting of beauty with use. The colors of the bags were extravagant, disciplined only by a "natural" taste. Blood-red and canary-yellow would interweave on one side: the other, in a quite different pattern, would bring together black, white, and green. But the most flamboyant part of the Cretan *pallikaria* was the head. It was straight-held, like the spine below it, and ornate. The eyes were intense, like the vital eyes on archaic Greek sculpture. The hair was almost invariably black. The true ornament, the jewel of the face, was a black moustache, again with Eastern origins, though standard wear in today's Greece. The Cretan moustaches were the most florid in Greece, emerging like thin, black hedge just above the upper lip. These were not elegant growths, thin, tooth-brush-shaped lines, or Hitlerian blocks under the nose. These Cretan moustaches were more exuberant, irrepressible overflows of virility.

The women walking on these streets were also handsome—

hardly beautiful. They were too strict—with the straightness and the strength of island women—to be beautiful, soft, or alluring. Their costumes were muted: black was the dominant color; the skirts were long and straight. These were women for the men of Crete: proud, courageous, reserved. Such, in fact, the Cretan people seemed (and seem) at first seeing. The eye insisted on this dangerous generalization. It insisted even when reminded by the mind of the reputation gained by the Cretans in antiquity, and never entirely lost, of being congenital liars, of having radically flawed natures. Reflection on that reputation was helpful. Lying was by no means the fault, to the ancient (or modern) Greeks, which it is considered in Anglo-Saxon countries. (Which is not to say that we lie less, only that we lie with a worse conscience.) After all, the ancient Greeks had a god—Hermes—for thieves and shrewd deceivers. They admired people who, like Odysseus, could prevaricate their ways out of danger. In the present-day Mediterranean, too, clever thieves are preferred to obtuse good citizens. In this context, this memory, I took the reputation of these Cretans as oblique, amused praise. When Odysseus wanted to tell a peculiarly extravagant tale he impersonated a Cretan, spoke out with the pure delight of art.

The qualities which struck me in Heraklion—Southern softness and sensuousness, manliness (and womanliness) of the kinds mentioned, and a certain informal *joie de vivre*—these qualities were at the centre of my imaginative experience of ancient Cnossos. I could not return the five kilometers from Cnossos, and enter Heraklion again, without being convinced of the continuity in character between ancient and modern Crete.

At Cnossos, of course, I found a palace, the relic of a luxurious civilization with which nothing in Crete today—or at other times in the past—can be compared. Yet the luxury at Cnossos, as well as

can be determined, was put to adequate aesthetic uses, and contributed to creating an aristocratic culture of beauty lovers. It was in
this aesthetic—in fact, sensuous—fullness of the palace that I
discovered its properly "Cretan" character.

The extensive and complex layout of the palace impressed me
first. It is imaginable, and believed by some, that the palace is in
the form of a Cretan labyrinth, of the kind which Daedalus built.
The structure seemed to me to have no form—or rather to be informal—but to have unity of conception. Dining halls, throne and
cult room, arms rooms, bedchambers, kitchens, and storerooms—
of which last there were many—drew themselves together into a
sumptuous whole. This was a place for royal living.

Penetrating inside, I found myself in a maze in which it was
quite possible to get lost. The surprisingly good condition of the
remains was due partly to Sir Arthur Evans' reconstruction, which,
along with the recently erected Stoa of Attalus in the Athenian
Agora, represents the most audacious of modern efforts to re-create
an ancient building. To Evans, I believe, I also owed the present
highly and beautifully restored condition of the frescoes, of which
copies were to be found throughout the restored palace, the origi-
nals being in the Heraklion museum. These frescoes concentrated
on the regal-aesthetic mood of the palace. They appeared to have
done this in organic relation to the whole living situation of Cnossos. The palace walls were as naturally and livably frescoed as the
walls of our houses are papered. In this way frescoes were able, far
more, say, than hung paintings, to enter vitally into life.

As I met those frescoes *in situ,* on walls situated between ornate,
red columns, and often surrounded by stylized floral motifs, the
paintings rose toward me with frightening immediacy. Theme and
color were one in them, proof that born painters created here. The
scene might be of a priest, of a man jumping over a bull—a popu-

lar athletic effort—or of inanimate nature—partridges, fish, lilies.
Art, religion, and sport were close in Minoan civilization, as they
were at Delphi and Olympia. The priests looked like athletes; the
athletes had a hieratic bearing. All was caught in aesthetic form. In
these frescoes the design and the color were bold: strong outlines,
movement in bodies; reds, blacks, whites. It was a demanding,
hard-hitting art, offering impressions of great vivacity and sensitive
naïveté. Nature seemed not to have been copied, but to have been
realized.

External nature, also, made a happy contribution to the scene at
Cnossos. As in Heraklion, the air was soft, the colors sensuous, nature generous—in fact, fertile—without being aggressive, or in any
sense tropical. Around Cnossos rolled low, calm hills with orchards
here and there. The palms of Heraklion were not visible here. It
was open country; there were well-cultivated fields. But the Southern quality of the island asserted itself. Cnossos itself conformed
the land to its own character, and itself to the land, the joys of
culture and of nature reinforcing one another with rare success.

The Minoan palace of Phaistos lies southwest, across Crete, from
Cnossos. Yet the forty-some miles between the two palaces are difficult. Going by bus, I found myself shaken until every joint in me
was loose. (Only the bus was closer to falling apart.) The world—
open and beautiful there—was tossed recklessly before restless and
unrestable eyes. The ride over such roads took three hours.

The fertility of the land was the strongest general impression
from the trip. Everywhere the hills were grass green, while from
the mainland and islands I had again grown used to bald, gray
hills, or at most to hills covered with shadowy pine forests. There
were many fruit orchards on Crete, and a far more elegant flora

than I met on the mainland. The sky was a thick, Prussian blue, in which cumulus clouds hung creamy and motionless. There was a strange languor over the island.

Phaistos itself was situated near the sea, on the long, rich Messara Plain, of which I had had a splendid view since descending from the mountainous central ridge of the island. That fertile stretch extended far to both east and west of Phaistos, and met the sea at the south. Fruits and vegetables were grown, on that plain, with an abundance unknown in the Greece I had left to the north. In these spots Crete was even more generous than the coasts of north Africa, to the south. The island lay, like Sicily, in a privileged position in the middle of the Aegean.

Phaistos itself is a palace in the style of Cnossos. Or, to be more exact, it is the remains of at least three palaces which succeeded one another on the spot; the last, and naturally now best preserved of those palaces, was destroyed around 1400 B.C. I again found, spread over a small plateau, buildings of every kind, from storehouses to throne room; enough to suggest that the palace must have been self-sufficient, a total living unit for a regional king and his retainers. This time there were no murals, no restored columns, none of the large storage jars which are disposed around the corridors and storerooms at Cnossos. All was stone colored, even gray, and very much left to its state as ruins. Yet the royal tone of the place had stayed.

Looking from the west I saw the broad entrance stairway into the palace. After I had entered and explored the palace, it seemed best to emerge and think my way back through, commencing with the royal entrance stairway. In this imagining, the complexity and the generosity of plan of Phaistos let themselves emerge almost symbolically. The rooms for thrones, dining, cooking, and storage stood

again, not, admittedly, with life in them, but as parts of an experienceable whole. In this awareness the continuing vitality of Phaistos
survived.

That kind of civilized experience, so different from the kind—
also civilized—which Cnossos offers, was also continuous with an
experience of nature. Particularly at Phaistos, where I sensed myself so far from any town, even from any quite familiar country,
the presence and the pressure of external nature were strong. It
seemed as though the sea, not far away, should be visible: I was
forever looking, irresistibly, toward the southern horizon—a long,
still conjunction of plain and sky, which appeared nearly to melt
away into water which was not quite visible. Nearly to that point of
mystery, for several miles, lay groves of olive trees, their leaves a
cool, cathartic green in the quiet air. To the northwest was Mount
Ida, where Zeus was born in a cave. To the east the Messara Plain
flowed fruitfully, a river of soil blocked out with fields of several
colors.

From arrival at Phaistos, I felt myself drawn not only toward the
sea but toward the olive trees before it. Certain places in nature, for
reasons difficult to determine, elicit an odd curiosity. Those long
rows of live trees were numinous, had power. Yet to experience
them was like experiencing a moral truth; you would have to be
among those trees to understand them, you would have had to encounter them. Onward!

The aesthetic mystery of Greek olive groves—at Amphissa, in
the Peloponnesus, on Crete—is inexhaustible. Those trees quickly
establish a single, dominant mood. It is a mood of calm, calm
which approaches and persuades the perceiver. Like the groves at
Amphissa, these Cretan groves were cool. Yet here they protected
from a stronger sun and a bluer sky. The shadows were conse-

quently darker and richer. Little trace of humanity crossed that protected ground. Nature was alone with itself, little disturbed by
invasive eyes.

So it was surprising to discover a town lodged in that stillness,
not far from the sea. The towns along the south coast of Crete, especially those farther west, are famous for their isolation and con-
servation of ancient ways of life. Few good roads lead to them, so
that even to other Greeks these places remain nearly unknown. In
the middle of the Phaistos olive groves I met just such a village. It
was little more than a clearing. Just outside it was an old, miniature
Byzantine church with several icons: the place was hardly spacious
enough for more than three worshippers. On the white stucco walls
of the first houses I saw bullet holes left from the last war, which
surged hard in that part of Crete. Within the village I at first saw
nobody. Everywhere were one-story, cream-colored houses and
stores. To find the citizens, I entered a store.

Several old men were talking, lost in the heavy shadow of a wine
store. In fact this village, and many of those around it, was known
for its wine and oil. The wine was sweet and fruity, like that malm-
sey which the Crusaders enthusiastically took back home with them.
(The name of which wine derives from Monemvasia, the small,
rocky island off the southeast coast of the Peloponnesus.) The men
in the wine store were, like many rural Greeks, both curious and
proud. They were probably avid to know my background, occupation, marital status, salary. No question, I knew, was too intimate
to be appropriate, and the person with reservations in answering
would quickly be set down as taciturn. I heard and answered the
questions. They were direct, hardly prefaced. Yet the questioners
lost no humanity in the process. I felt that they were contented with
their own situation, curious out of exuberance, essentially reaching

forward for a world. Another world. But they were proud of their own world. I found it hypnotic just to touch that world. What must it mean to have passed a life there?

The emotion-awakening power of Crete, its accessibility to romantic feeling, kept assailing me on this trip. Cretan myths have that power. So have the chief Minoan remains, which carried me back to a time exciting by its mere age, not to mention its aesthetic vigor. Even nature in Crete was different. On the mainland of Greece nature frequently cooperated with art, enhancing the effect of temples or Byzantine churches. Some artforms, like the temple of Sunium, appear to "elevate" nature into greater clarity and significance. Very seldom, though, does that nature exist wholly outside of a controlled aesthetic relation: sea, sky, mountains present themselves either in bondage to art, or as inwardly accessible to an artistic eye, from an artistic point of view. In another sense, Greek nature is disciplined, concordant to human faculties. Some Cretan nature was wilder. It asked more of the wildness in me, in my feelings.

Eastern Crete proved to be without large towns. It was a region of villages set deeply in nature, against a landscape than which none in Greece can be less tamed. From a plane, I suppose, that part of the island would appear almost totally desolate. It was heavily forested, the coasts were inhospitable, and mountains rose blockingly here and there. As in south-central Crete, there were few visitors. Again, though, this lack could not be attributed to lack of worthwhile things to see.

Agios Nikolaos, on the Bay of Mirabello, is a pure town. I reached it, typically enough, by a jolting bus ride which far exceeded in danger the ride to Phaistos. For east from Heraklion we had to take a coast road under which, at the foot of a vertiginous cliff, lay the sea. If, as I suppose is generally possible, and was true in my case, the driver is sleepy—his nodding head reflecting itself in the large mirror before him—or if he is simply very talkative, such a bus ride can be emotionally enervating. Agios Nikolaos was gladly seen, and the bus joyfully abandoned. By contrast with the trip, the town was pure peace. It had the usual white-walled, narrow-streeted aspects. Domes of a few Byzantine churches were visible. And not far down the street, from the centre of town, spread the invariantly turquoise Bay of Mirabello, with a few small boats parked against its quai. Under the sun the bay glistened as a single surface, almost as a fine mosaicked gold which only the sun elicited. That beckoning surface covered the fish, which swam like forms in a frieze at Cnossos: on those swimmers much of the economy of Agios Nikolaos depended. Otherwise the town depended on oil and fruits for its own sustenance and for sale. Fruit sellers propped their carts of oranges, grapes, and figs at the side of the street and patiently waited to make money.

In all of this, of course, little of the untameness of some Cretan nature was apparent. Nor, as far as Agios Nikolaos went, did that natural untameness ever, for me, become more than an unhampered freedom and ebullience in nature, something experienceable at the approach to Heraklion, and on the Messara Plain, and there already different from nature on the Greek mainland. Yet that natural freedom was impressive at Agios Nikolaos. In the mornings a joyful sun intruded through the shutters of the hotel rooms. It picked up the items in those rooms—clocks, draped clothes, the wood of the floor—and called them to existence, as the sun has done for each of us before as children, when it climbed to the window and woke us.

Outside the hotel, the grass was covered with dew, the trees were almost unpleasantly verdant, the bay was again and again turquoise. There is an intensity of nature everywhere in Greece, but it assumes an unquestionable difference in Crete. There was a kind of sensuous gaiety which reflected itself in the art of Cnossos and for which— much as we talk of the *Heiterkeit* and *Allgemeinheit* of ancient mainland Hellas—there is no counterpart in the art we call "classical" Greek. There is something more austere about external nature on the mainland.

For me, that intuition about Cretan nature was strengthened by an excursion out from Agios Nikolaos. The view from the road along the Bay of Mirabello was blinding. That bay was not more intense in color than the Aegean usually is: but Mirabello was gayer, brighter, even foaming to whitecaps which jittered and leapt in the sun. Across the road the hills rose, heavily coated with trees —oaks, pines, patches of olive grove. Grass was conspicuous, damp and fertile. The sky was a moist, rich blue.

Not far from Agios Nikolaos, a few kilometers inland, was the site of Lato, which was once—in the ninth century B.C.—one of the most powerful cities in Crete, but which is now only an imposing ruin enjoying the view down onto the Bay of Mirabello. Lato's remains—houses, shops, terraces—constitute one of the few significant witnesses to sub-Mycenean culture, that is to the post-Minoan culture which had Mycenae as its centre.

I reached the ruined Lato, that day, at the top of a steep, rocky hill. Climbing toward the acropolis, I found it necessary to cross several of the terrasses which supported the old city. These piles of stone were badly fallen across the paths where a people once regularly climbed their hill. The bulk of the city was on top of the hill, in a small basin of streets and house foundations, from which I enjoyed, and I suppose people have always enjoyed, an unusually broad panorama of the long-sided bay stretching islandlessly to the north. The land below the hill seemed to lean forward without effort until it vanished in that inviting blueness.

The clearest measure of the character of Cretan nature came out in precisely that experience of Lato. There the past was not melancholy. The wind blowing across the stones on that hill did not seem a negative, reaping force, an image of time which wipes out human communities. Nor were reflections, philosophical encounters with the past, in order. Rather past and present seemed essentially one, part of the appreciative life of the senses, for which the sense-awakening joy of the moment was enough.

Asia Minor: The Old Greece Lives

I RETURNED TO Chios from Crete during the night, rising early to see the gray mound of the island not far off the ship. It was a blustery, nervous morning. I landed at eight, and hurried to arrange for the passage to Asia Minor. In the small, smoky, poster-lined room of the shipping agent I confirmed what I had feared: that the transportation to Cesme, which was clearly visible from Chios, would be extravagantly expensive. The cunning boatowner had a racket. He smiled at my helplessness as I gave him the round-trip fare. It was, if I ever saw one, a monopoly needing to be cracked.

On the ride across I was alone with a single passenger and the pilot, who had the disconcerting habit of coming out on deck to talk with us. The sea was still. I sat on a small bench at the prow, watching our smoke dissolve in the milk-blue air. The coast grew clearer, like an object in a focussing camera lense. Our boat was oddly still on the still sea, so that our destination seemed to move toward us.

Cesme itself came like an unassertive romantic painting. It was a small gray coast town, constructed mostly of stucco and dull stone.

On the rise behind it stood a decrepit minaret, the dome of its mosque half visible. The town itself seemed to consist of irregular rows of low houses, divided by cobblestone streets which appeared and vanished in my eye as our caïque manoeuvred about in the small harbor. The waterfront itself was simple. A shapeless tollhouse building snuggled up to the quai; a couple of coffeehouses stood nearby, as waiting rooms. I carried my bags into one of the cafés, and sat down to wait for the bus to Smyrna. It came gradually over me, as I waited, that I was in fact in Turkey, the Turkey of romantic imagination, of which Lamartine wrote a history, and Delacroix painted the colors. Unshaven, slack men, whose bones seemed scarcely to hold them in their metal-backed chairs, sat over eternal sweet coffee, and tossed dice in a monotonous, echoing ritual over the marble tables. I drank water and watched.

I almost missed the bus to Smyrna, in spite of my attention to the time. Looking up, I saw the old, yellow crate blundering down the road toward my café. The bus had started from the wrong place, at least from a secondary terminal: that is, from the front of another café. I raced out. Several of the old men hurried out with me, cursing under their breath at the unreliability of the bus service, and supplicating the preoccupied bus driver to stop. He did.

I climbed into the rear of the completely full bus. (It was puzzling that so many people were leaving Cesme, the starting point of the bus line, that noon.) With superb energy the passengers made room for me. Several chickens were squashed into the corner, old women dressed in black were crowded even closer together, and a nook for me appeared in the backmost row, which ran the width of the bus. I crawled through the row and sat down, already causing and suffering discomfort.

The bus moved cumbrously on, creaking and ploughing through the overcast day, over the rut-lined road. The people around me took up their conversations again. There were several soldiers and some fat women near me. The occupants of the front half of the bus were scarcely visible from where I sat. Open, voluble talk came from the mid-regions of the bus. On rare occasions I caught sight of the driver himself: usually he was turning to talk with someone sitting near him. The landscape passed like half-seen background in an old film. My rear was soon sore and my back stiff.

Efforts at verbal friendship with me were made, but they failed. I appeared to share no language, almost no words, with these people. We were thrown back on an elemental relationship which characteristically intimidates the Anglo-Saxon, while it stimulates the Greek or Turk. Smiles followed words. Active attempts were made to win me with tidbits: *loukoumia,* pieces of bread, drinks of water. I took some bits, and finessed others. A good deal of talking about me took place. It was, I believe, transparently enthusiastic, although I could sense that unsatisfied curiosity was hampering the complete enjoyment of me.

The real bridge between inarticulate beings was created an hour later. We stopped at a small town which closely resembled a Greek village. Small, white stucco houses lined the road on both sides. Several passengers got off, some got on. We sat for five minutes, waiting. Then two of the soldiers, previously on my right, came back to the bus, carrying large strands of fresh, purple figs which were dripping with clear water. The men got in, and sat down; they were strong, swarthy, twenty-five years old. One of them smiled triumphantly at me, as though to say that now we could do business. He handed me the largest strand of figs, while around him the passengers beamed; now it was up to me. I smiled back, and, taking the gift, immediately began to eat. It was futile to try to respond adequately; the gift was too genuine. The purer the gift you receive, I think, the more it throws you back on bare humanity, the less it permits a socially conventional response. The figs were sweet and fresh, and I hoped that the others could see my pleasure. I strengthened my hope with a round of fruity smiles.

Then I knew, as we rattled through the afternoon, that there was an ancient Greek nerve pulsing in the bus. Guest friendship, with its elemental ground in human nature, was always a distinguishing expression of the Hellenic spirit.

Coming from the south you cannot see Smyrna dramatically, but there is drama in the event. That old city was one of the most prosperous entrepôts of antiquity, important both to Greece and to Rome. Its importance, as one of the chief ports of the eastern Mediterranean, has lasted to this day. You can hardly approach Smyrna without re-experiencing, anticipantly, once-awakened feelings about Levantine traders and shiploads of rugs.

The beauty of the city, like that of Naples, appears best from the harbor; from there Smyrna's splendid layout among hills is evident, and the bay's embrace of the city seems only an extension of your own outreaching vision. But from the south you must cross the surrounding hills to reach the city: the perfect perspective is destroyed.

From my first entrance to Smyrna, consequently, I remember crowded streets and a hotel. It was early evening when I came to the Karavanserai. I felt my aloneness. Beloved fellow passengers had left the bus long before, at many small towns now far away. The bus, which had seemed a last contact with Greece itself, with a language and place I knew, was parked and still. The bus driver had pointed me toward my hotel, and I had gone off down the formal, broad, unreal boulevard. It was hard to accept the existence of Smyrna at dusk.

The hotel was large and still. Before me, as I entered, was a dark,

narrow corridor, terminating in what can best be called a reception cabinet. Behind an open, sliding window, under the half-light of an electric bulb, a man was filing papers. He was fat and torpid, though he managed a thin smile as I approached him: first he spoke in Turkish. Then readily seeing my Americanness—my inescapable aura—he brought out the inevitable words of English and we completed negotiations for a room.

It was darkish upstairs, too, in the large antiquated corridor. My room was in a corner, looking out onto the street by which I had come. I put down my bag and went out onto the small balcony. I had asked to have a bath prepared, and was waiting for the fat man, who seemed to be a factotum, to tell me the water was ready. Soon there was a knock. Opening the door, I could see two women swaying away from me down the corridor. One of them turned, and smiled. I closed the door.

A little later, I went a floor higher to bathe. The bathroom itself —curiously antiquated enough to deserve a separate essay—was a considerable distance from the staircase, down a murky corridor. The area had a subterranean air. Off of dark side halls branched darker rooms, modestly furnished. I noticed that many of the doors were partially open. There were women in most of the rooms. Someone giggled behind a closed door.

I bathed, and returned through the same murkiness. There was more giggling.

When I went out, after dinner, the old streets of the city were pullulating with human bodies. The distinction between street and sidewalk had been abandoned. People of all ages walked, chattered, and traded recklessly across the entire width of the street. This activity did not eliminate traffic, though it hindered it. The cars drove slowly, brushing coattails, honking steadily, carrying their cursing owners slowly home.

The sensuousness of the scene was Hellenic: vital, colorful, worldly. Yet it was Hellenic in that complex way characteristic of contemporary Asia Minor. Mosques were conspicuous, the language was Turkish, the formal aspect of shop windows, dress, and architecture impressed their slight difference from the Hellenic mood. But the Greek spirit lived there. Well it might. The coast of Asia Minor had been, in greater or less degree, continuously settled by Greeks since the beginning of the first millenium B.C. The extent of settlement, at any given time, is hard to judge. In antiquity there were many Greek settlers. Subsequently, Turkish, Syrian, and Greek populations have been thoroughly intermixed in Asia Minor. Since 1453 the welcome of Greeks in Turkey has been limited. (With Cyprus between the two countries, now, what possibility is there for improvement?) In 1922, as the result of continuing, bitter hostilities between Greece and Turkey, there was an exchange of populations between the two countries. Greeks went "home" to create, and settle in, impoverished suburbs of Athens, in places like Nea Smyrne. But even then they left their spirit, a few of their fellows, and many material traces behind them. Their spirit has remained, and with it the sensuous mood of pre-Christian Hellenic Asia Minor. It was that mood, incarnated history, through which I was walking in the crowded streets.

Vital remains of Greek antiquity lie outspread along the west coasts of Turkey like the limbs of a single, dismembered creature. Pergamum, an ancient Greek city, abounds with meaningful vestiges, which can be reached in a three-hour bus ride north from Smyrna. Again, as in the approach to Smyrna from the south, bodily discomfort is the price of spiritual pleasure.

It was my good fortune to be shown the ruins of Pergamum by a man who both loved and understood them. He was the archaeologist in residence there, and devoted his time to me. Manifold as the ruins are, certain features asserted themselves as most characteristic, and as implying the whole.

That whole, to be sure, is vast and complex. It covers a wide area. At the centre is a rocky acropolis, covered—both on top and on its sides—with ruins: temple, library, palazzi, altar. Around the flat lands below the acropolis spread other stones; baths, agora, amphitheater. Much is still unidentified, I learned, while most of the city of ancient Pergamum, as distinct from its cult areas, is presumed to lie buried under the modern city of Bergama, which adjoins the ruins. The time span of the Pergamene ruins is also considerable. The oldest, it seems, can be dated to the third century B.C. From that time to our day the surrounding area has been actively and continuously occupied. Pergamum was an important seat of early Christianity, one of the so-called Seven Churches. Modern Bergama is active industrially. Its foundations are pre-Christian Greek. Much of its superstructure is constituted by the walls of a small Byzantine Church. The top of the walls, the doming, and the interior are now elements of an actively used mosque.

Within the spatial-temporal whole of Pergamum, certain elements forced themselves on me with particular, almost symbolic, force. These symbols were clustered about, and pointed toward, the spirit of cultured Hellenic sensuousness.

My friend and I went first to the acropolis, driving to its peak up a winding, sharp-curved dirt road. The day was fresh and clear; as we rose, the land spread itself farther in all directions, an outrolling, multicolored pattern. The world looked passive below us, as though invoking our vision. Yet even more invoking, once we reached the top, was the stone-benched, deep-sided Greek theater, down into which we looked as though into a funnel. I fell eyelong, almost headlong, into that disciplined vortex.

We were near the centre point of the uppermost tier of benches, but we were far from the orchestra. Yet, as is usually true of Greek public buildings, this theater was well made. The orchestra was conspicuous and attracting, a target of vision which seemed, once I had the feel of it, to reduce the rest of the visible world to a background. In this case the rolling, placid landscape, which as usual had at Pergamum been drawn carefully into the experienceable orbit of the theater, hung like a fostering mood about the peripheries of the eye. I felt, rather than saw, nature. Acoustical effects had been equally well managed. Slight sounds echoed down or up the steep cleft hill. In the highest tier a line spoken in normal voice from the orchestra is audible. Sounds acquired uncommon worth. I spoke and listened carefully. Nowhere has live nature—hills, rocks, landscapes—been better disciplined in the service of art than in the finest Greek theaters: Pergamum is one of them.

Near the theater, on the acropolis, lie the foundations of the once splendid and ornate Temple of Zeus, which was constructed by Eumenes II, King of Pergamum, in the second century B.C. The theme of the expressionist sculptures of that temple's frieze is the battle of Zeus and Athena against the snake-legged giants. The sculptural work, the remains of which are in Berlin, is in high relief, and is as dramatically tense as the Laocoön. Yet it has, like the Laocoön, the imaginative strictness of great baroque sculpture.

Feeling the presence at Pergamum of the absent supporting base and of the absent surmounting frieze is not easy. I turned from the theater to the well-arranged temple foundations, and tried to reconstruct, first, the high base around which the frieze ran, then the porticoed wings above it, sacred to Zeus. As mortar to this reconstruction, awe was needed. The remaining sculpture from the tem-

ple embodied the feeling of the victory of civilization over barbarism, a motif which preoccupied Greek experience. The whole
work, finally, needed to be seen in incandescent marble, surrounded
by a matching complex of cult buildings.

This difficult effort in the mind, far as it surely was from an accurate realization, perhaps suggested the maturity of sensuous experience which was embodied in, and elicited by, the structures of
Pergamene civilization. The theater and the temple were both high
aesthetic achievements, enriching to the senses, which refined themselves in such art. Yet both works, in their respective functions,
subdued themselves to a spirit which filled them like a theme. The
theater was experienced as the frame of dramas, "classical" Greek
dramas, for which an ideal sensuous surrounding was required. The
frieze and altar to Zeus, as experienced, closed about a never attain-
able, but always present, sense of wonder at the power and beauty
of civilization's triumph over barbarism.

The attention to fine experience, which I found in many of the
grand structures of Pergamum, appeared, in a different form, in the
Asclepieion on the plain below the acropolis. That building, of a
type found throughout Greek lands, is dedicated to the god of healing and was, next to the one at Epidaurus, the largest sanctuary of
Asclepius in the Greek world. As such, it gives insight into one of
the chief popular cults of antiquity, a cult in which "ordinary"
Greeks and Romans sought health on this side of the grave, as they
sought beneficent immortality in the worship of Dionysus.

Among the scattered remains of that sanctuary, with its altars,
chapels, and sleeping rooms, is what we might call a psychiatric
ward. There is one room in which, it is known from inscriptions,
disturbed worshippers could sleep after having undergone the necessary purifications. There they went to sleep peacefully and deeply.
Priests of the god served as resident psychiatrists. They, or even the

god, would come to the patient at night, and attempt to cure him
with dreams; presumably, that is, through subconscious suggestion.

Enough of these techniques is known to broaden, even farther,
our respect for the civilized attention of Pergamene culture to human experience. It is the first mark of an authentic culture that it
builds "spiritually" on the basic sensuous life of its citizens.

Some Turkish popular music has elemental force. The next day I
found myself walking toward such a field of force, in the old part
of Smyrna. Out of a small door poured long, fluid, repeated wails:
the "long wail," in fact, which Kemal Atatürk tried to expurgate
from Turkish music, knowing well how "unprogressive" and "un-
modern" the spirit of such singing is. The fez went, but the wail
stayed. I paid, and went in.

The room was bare and ugly; it looked like a temporarily rented
revival-meeting hall. In the front was a wooden platform, with
seven folding chairs and seven "performers" on them. The hall itself was lined with chairs, in fifteen or twenty rows. A few soldiers
were sitting in the middle of the room, a few older men in the
back. The poor lighting contributed to the extreme dinginess of the
scene. Pear-shaped, unshaded bulbs glared from the ceiling. I sat
down a few chairs away from the soldiers, who turned and smiled
enthusiastically at me.

The music rose. There were three women and four men on the
stage, all seated; nearly as many performers as listeners. All the artists except two women had instruments, *bouzoukia* or guitars. They
were playing strenuously, in harmony with one of the women, who
was singing, or wailing. The music seemed endless, the winding
and unwinding of a single, eternal, melodic chord. In waves the
music reached crescendos, nearly ended, then began again. It was
fast, harsh, emotional. The men centred their playing on the *chan-*

teuse; she sat impassively among them, her voice rising and falling, sometimes in words, sometimes in a controlled wail. She rarely moved; plump, short, dressed in a simple house dress, she sat like an ancient Magna Mater, or that Cybele, who was (and still is) the patron goddess of Smyrna. Occasionally her breasts shook; the soldiers stamped and grinned.

As the artistic monotony continued, my attention wandered. The music was fascinating, but no more than that. Yet the soldiers were transported. I think it was no lewd pleasure they were taking, though sexual it was. They seemed involved in the whole musical occasion, and with Cybele only as she fitted in. Her sexual fulness was dramatically part of the sexual energy of the whole performance, which sounded progressively more like the eternal, procreative voice of nature, rising and falling in the appropriate seasons, but never stopping. It grew obsessive. I had to call my own halt, at last. I nodded to the soldiers. Then I left the endless music and the soldiers, or rather the rite and the devotees, and went out into the finite social world.

The finitude of that social world, and at the same time the effort of modern Turkey to modernize itself, were strongly revealed to me the next morning. I appreciated how firm a countermovement to antiquity was underway in that ancient country, and how partial a description of Turkey could be given by emphasizing its Hellenic ancientness.

One of my severest difficulties in Smyrna had been in trying to buy envelopes. I could not find the proper word in my dictionary, or, if I had found it, I could not pronounce it right. With the help of a retired major, who knew a dozen words of English, I finally succeeded. After I had mailed my letters, I sat down in a small, neat park near the water. It was a breezy morning; around the plot of flowers at the park's centre there was dew on the grass. A small bust, some stiffly immortalized politician, gleamed on its pedestal among the zinnias. I looked out to sea, where a few small boats were manoeuvring. There were only a few people around.

It was evident, though, that others were coming into the vicinity, that the park was less empty. Middle-aged couples were standing about, waiting. Then band music became audible. From up the street, toward the centre of Smyrna, came the noise of drums, flutes, and bugles. A martial spirit on the still, blue air. Soon a group of public musicians came briskly into the park and took up positions near the sidewalk along the coast. They were dressed in close, military-type uniforms. Now the benches were nearly full. A concert was on.

I sat through a half-hour program of band music. There was a rightness about such hearty music at this time; it was the kind of program you might hear in the *Kursaal* of a Swiss city in summer. The audience was festive, if a little stiff. They seemed thoroughly responsive. I looked at a book for a few minutes, but felt conspicuous and paid attention again.

After a while I decided to leave. Surely the concert was nearly over. Glancing up, I saw a couple of men rising to the right of me. Without looking around, or noticing the change in the character of the music, I rose and began to walk away. Before I had gone ten steps I felt strong hands clamped on my shoulders. Turning, I saw a dark, tall Turk glowering at me, his face agitated. He was speaking loudly, much more insistently than the music. I turned, into the face of the music, and saw that all the careful listeners were standing at attention, stiff and strict as statues. Then I knew. This last piece was the national anthem. The giant at my shoulder wanted me to show respect. Close to him I stood quietly until the ceremonious music ended. The giant did not smile as we left. The compul-

sive spirit of nationalism was on the group. The air blew clean and sterile across the tidy park.

Three hours by train to the south of Smyrna lies Ephesus, the ancient city with which the worship of Artemis was associated throughout antiquity. Kybele, important in Smyrna, may simply have been one of many forms adopted by Artemis, who in "Asian" lands was deeply involved with sexual forces. Our conventional picture of Artemis as a virginal huntress, chastely running the mountains in moonlight, with her bands of virgins, appears to be quite misleading. It is a picture first drawn for us by the settlers of mainland Greece, members, as Gilbert Murray has said, of a "patriarchal, monogamous system" of society. But even on the Greek mainland Artemis remained a protectress of wild creatures and of childbirth. That is, she continued to be concerned with fostering life. Long before, in Phrygia, or in Crete, where Artemis first appears, she has this same concern. Yet she is there far closer to the passionate forces of procreation. Sculptures show her covered with breasts. Legends suggest her animal, bearlike, nature. She reminds at times of earlier vegetation goddesses, or of Demeter, with whom she was occasionally associated.

Artemis of the Ephesians, the most widely worshipped Artemis of Asia Minor, was the object of a long, refined cult. She appears to have had both earth-mother and virginal traits, to have been, if such a thing can exist, a composite divinity. As such, she sponsored worship from which an important cult of the Virgin Mary grew.

One legend holds that Mary was buried at Ephesus, which, like Pergamum, was one of the important centres of early Christianity. The Church of the Virgin, at Ephesus, is the object of large, annual pilgrimages, and the centre of a cult which shows with unique clarity how deeply Greek religion has influenced Christianity. The

Mary worshipped at Ephesus has many traits of the Ephesian Artemis, and found a ready ground for worship there precisely because
of this similarity. The main common trait of the two goddesses is
precisely the paradoxical union of motherhood with virginity.

This rich mother-virgin model for experience is a characteristic
product of the Asia Minor coast. Artemis becomes a kind of re-
fined, sensuous symbol in which the land and the civilization of
that coast find expression. It is a measure, too, of the richness of
that symbol that it could coalesce with the image of the Mother of
Christ. The finest efforts of sense-refinement in Asia Minor were of
world-historical significance.

The ruins of Ephesus suggested, to me, this same mood of sense-
refinement. Those ruins breathed purity. Yet, though less dramatic
than the stones of Pergamum, they were the ruins of a worldly,
cultivated city.

To describe those ruins in any detail here would be useless. In
many ways the ruins of Ephesus seemed to resemble those of Pergamum. At both sites the chief public buildings of a prosperous,
independent city were preserved: temples, theater, agoras, libraries,
and remarkably intact networks of streets and houses. At Ephesus
there was no conspicuous acropolis. The city was built in the rich
Caÿster Plain, at a confluence of three rivers.

But the spirit of preserved Ephesus was distinctive. It was one of
peaceful succumbing to nature's supremacy. In this, the ruins of
Ephesus fulfilled romantic expectations better than those of Pergamum. Everywhere at Ephesus grass grew over the stones, dimin-
ishing their energy, softening them. The public buildings were
turned in upon themselves with strange passivity. The theater,

which at Pergamum was so dynamic, was at Ephesus calm and quiet. The Ephesian streets were time heavy. The foundations of the temples there, even of the huge Temple to Artemis, showed less inner striving toward their original wholeness, less desire to support columns and architraves, than did the foundations at Pergamum.

It struck me that the pure passivity of this mood was realized by the library, which, like the one at Pergamum, was important. It is thought that the Ephesian library was the collection of Celsus, an erudite Roman writer, known now chiefly for his work on medicine. As the building now stands you see the small stone cubicles in which the rolled parchments were stored, as our books are stored on library shelves. There is little more to see now in that ancient library. It preserves, though, an easy mood; as though the ghosts of cultured browsers had never been expurgated from that small space of air. Of browsers, indeed, whose richest awareness went into the worship of Artemis, in whose onward-living cult the main potency of ancient Ephesus resided. And from whose cultivated daily life only the quiet, dying vestiges remain.

Scattered along the coasts of Smyrna's wide bay are a number of suburbs. They can be reached either by bus or by boat; a regular ferry service goes back and forth from the Smyrna quai. On my next-to-last day in that city I took the ferry, in the late afternoon, out into the bay. I wanted to see the city again, as it should be seen.

The impetus had come from a Turkish acquaintance in Smyrna, a doctor to whom I had been given a letter of introduction. On one of my first days there he had shown me winding streets, a bazaar; and had taken me in a trolley car up to the hills behind the city. I had been impressed by his face, as well as by what he showed me. He was proud of the place. Its vitality pleased him, and me through

him. He had a large, white forehead, stern eyes, and a modern pro-
fessional man's manner. Yet I felt him oddly a part of the upswell-
ing energies of the city. He had had a special goal in mind, that
morning, a café overlooking the bay. There we had sat down, and
ordered large glasses of yogurt, a wonderful freshness eaten with
spoons. Below us the business in the city and on the long, Greece-
ward stretching harbor had seemed suddenly calmed, diminutively
beautiful. We had left those energies ten minutes before; now we
were looking down on them with Olympian peace. It was the contrast my friend had wanted. We talked; and knew the moment for
its rarity. It was soon over. The doctor's last advice had been:
"Take a ferry out into the bay; you'll understand Smyrna even better from there."

The boat, which he had recommended, was full with people going home from the city. It was a commuting crowd, masculine,
tired, preoccupied, I thought, with the changing lights on the water, and the stillness of blank inner life. Group by group they disembarked, the boat being tied against the local piers one by one.
The bay was just a large pond. Smyrna was never more than fifteen
minutes distant from us.

Soon the ferry was nearly empty. A handful of people moved on
the decks, or sat smoking in corners. The sun was setting; inch by
inch it toppled into the extinguishing sea, leaving long threads of
fire behind it in the blue, opaque sky. As the ferry turned toward
home, I saw that the glow of the sun was fully on Smyrna, seeping
into the visible nooks of the city. The land before us was held in
that copper-red light; a potent unity held hills, coast, and city in a
single grasp. I felt myself go forth, with my seeing, until I was
hardly aware of my bodily presence on the boat.

The city, old sophisticated Smyrna, returned to the earth. At the
same time, nature rose up to the city. Man and nature were one. In

this instant both were part of a single, distinction-blurring beauty, a beauty as sensuously pure as Ephesian Artemis. I supposed that the vision would fade quickly. Asia Minor was complex. But the old unity of Hellenic Asia Minor had been imaged for an instant. My friend had been right.

Mount Athos: God's Summit

FILLED WITH a certain sense of fullness I began the last stage of the journey. It was time to be completing the circle. With growing excitement I realized that between me and my way back lay Mount Athos. That I was to fulfill that long-time debt before starting back across Jugoslavia.

By boat from Smyrna it was not long to Samothrace, then to Kavalla, then down into the Chalcidice. Upon entering that peninsula, the pure ambience of external nature began to close around me. I realized this strongly at the beginning of my trip onto Athos itself. The impression began with the donkey ride from Hierissos to Tripiti. Hierissos was the last town in Chalcidice north of the Athos boundary; Tripiti was the one-house port on the west side of the peninsula, from which began the boat ride to Dafne, the gateway to Athos. I left the simple—*sauber aber einfach* says the *Baedeker* wisely—hotel in Hierissos at five-thirty, with two other travellers and our donkeys. It was Good Friday morning, the middle of April, early spring. Around us the Chalcidian landscape showed its peculiar virginity. It was essentially folded gray rock; but rock cov-

ered with low green bushes, some dark and prickly—like holly—
others with tender light leaves, and a third bush—which I subsequently saw all over the peninsula—heavy with small ear-shaped
yellow flowers. Such a vision of gray rock under green bush with
occasional touches of flower brightness was to remain as the chief
visual impression of Athos. With the sea always somewhere near
as the scene's true ground; and that second sea, the sky, strangely
flooding light on everything out of its blue opaqueness.

From where we rode, Mount Athos itself was not yet visible. It
was bound to come soon, at some turn of a road, or sudden rise.
We could already see much of the coast of the Athian peninsula
stretched fingerlike out to the south. Across the bay to the west was
Sithonia, the central of the three prongs of the Chalcidice. Almost
no one lives there. An austere accident of rock, which like Athos
might have had twenty holy cloisters on it. But which lies instead in
another kind of purity.

My mind asked: what could not have been made pure in this
Chalcidian landscape? My feelings agreed: nothing. I rode on in
this comfortable mood for a while. Half an hour, perhaps. Then,
halfway to Tripiti, as I was feeding my eyes peacefully on nature,
I saw something which made me think.

It was Good Friday: nearly the spiritual centre of the Christian
year. In Greece this season is hallowed both by great gravity and
by great gaiety. Many preparations are made. One of them—a national custom—is to sacrifice a sheep to be eaten on Easter day at
the end of fasting. The sheep elected for slaughter usually have
their heads dyed red: this designates them as chosen.

In a stream bed to the right of our path there was a line of
twenty red-headed, prone sheep on the sand. Some clearly had their
throats slit, and were dead, though not quite motionless. These had
stripes of scarlet blood on their clay-red dyed throats. But at the end

of the line nearest me—perhaps twenty-five yards away—were four sheep which were alive. They were held down by two men who were kneeling on the sheep's hind legs; one of them was working to finish the killing. Off to the side a third person was grabbing the hind leg of a fat ram which was trying to elude him. It was all astonishing. We had come suddenly on this strenuous scene in the middle of the fresh dawn. I was struck by the grotesqueness of the red-headed sheep, of the neat line their corpses made, tucked belly to back on the sand, and by the routine way the men were attending to business. That was all. We passed them quickly. And were folded again into the still peace of dawn. Almost as though the slaughter had been dreamed.

The donkeys jogged on for a while. Then slowly the question began to rise in me, insistently, surprisingly: Why am I so little shocked by what I just saw? Where is my delicacy of feeling about the killing of innocent creatures? "I'd rather kill a man than a hawk, if it weren't for the penalties." That strong line from Robinson Jeffers had often impressed me. But my donkey was jogging along, along, now. And I couldn't recover the feeling of outraged innocence. Why?

Something in the morning had made that sheep killing seem in place, seem to belong. The mood of the morning's nature was innocent, spontaneous, pure. Surprisingly, the same mood had seemed to surround the slaughter. It had had the purity of a sacramental killing about it. In fact, as I thought of it, there seemed to be almost a blend of piety with savagery in that pure natural act. This was a reflection I could understand better later.

I worked on it then for a while, though. Until we reached Tripiti, in fact, an hour and a half after setting out from our hotel. There the Aegean was beside us again. Slapping and muttering

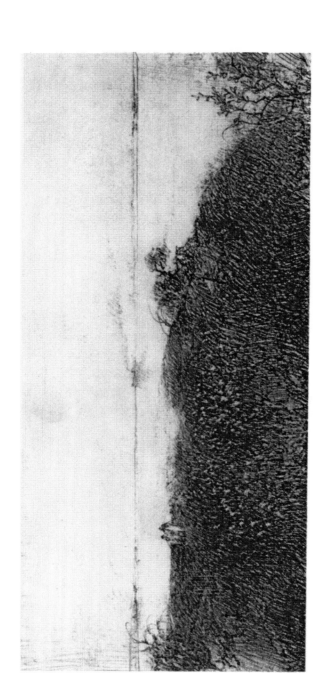

against the white sand. The water was brilliant today: close to shore
it was diaphanous and turquoise; huge rocks on the bottom looked
as delicate as sea shells. And opposite us, as light as a thought on
the sea, lay the island of Amouliane. Farther than ever to the south
stretched the winding peninsula of Athos. Gray-green, rising: half
visible toward its end was the lower part of the mountain itself.
Still no peak in sight.

Beside the little quai at Tripiti we found our caïque: a tough,
cramped little boat. We jumped in promptly, feeling—or at least
I attributed the feeling to us all—that this boat was taking us far,
to a new land. Then we putted off, cleaving the otherwise motionless water, and left nothing but a frothy wake as our farewell to
the unholy world.

It was three hours by caïque from Tripiti to the port of Athos:
Dafne. Although we passed the border of the monks' republic—a
broken stone wall—and saw three monasteries in the hills along the
way, our morning continued to be wholly in nature. A kind of incu-
bation ride, before we would emerge on the holy soil itself. Coast,
sea, sky: we were being bathed and purified in these elements, so as
to be ready for the coming experience. Or so it seemed.

It was good to see the tiny harbor and town of Dafne. The holy
community at last. Here was our goal, or the threshold to it. I didn't
know how little this would mean leaving pure nature behind.

Landing on the coast of Athos with your first visit ahead is like
confronting a new, exciting idea, only half imaginable. In both
cases your mind is stirred by prospects which allure; but allure
vaguely. You can feel this kind of excitement in Dafne.

The town is simply one street, two blocks long, lined with little
dry-goods stores, a tollhouse, a post office, a barbershop and a cou-

ple of restaurants and coffee shops. Along the small wharf small
boats—caïques, fishing boats, rowboats—are lined. The pace is
slow.

On this stage walked three different kinds of actors, who sorted
oddly with one another, and made their impressions. First there
were the monks: this was their home, their state. They wore long
black gowns, and black hats; each monk was bearded, and had let
his hair grow long. Excess head hair was either made into a bun in
back or folded under the hat. There was no such thing as excess
beard; the more the better. These strong, stark figures were the main
actors in Dafne, as they went their businesslike way, doing jobs for
their monasteries or getting their own provisions. Then there were
the nonmonastic Greek residents of Athos: employees of the toll
office, owners of the shops and restaurants, fishermen, policemen,
and others. These men led a regular secular life except—the huge
qualification—that they were without women. For no woman, in
fact no female being—cow, hen, or nanny goat—was allowed on
the holy peninsula. And it was fairly clear that these Greek civil-
ians didn't feel completely at home there. They were subdued, for
Greeks, and behaved rather listlessly, as the uncommitted often do
in the homes of the committed. Finally there were the tourists. I
met few of these. (Seven Germans, one Swede.) These were the
men with cameras. There goes one now; arriving. He is curious,
holds a map, carries a knapsack a little too heavy for him. There is
another; leaving. He is dirty, tired, spiritually alert, and anxious to
get home. Both of these men are conspicuous actors here.

The effect of this scene at Dafne was exciting. I felt many things
at first. One was: here, in this border station between two worlds,
walked men who were committed to a world completely different
from mine. As I looked at them I asked myself: are these men in

special touch with divinity? I saw them with a mixture of awe and alarm. I also wondered: Where are their monasteries? Why are they in Dafne? How can they endure this heat?

Then I started out onto the steep path into the hills above Dafne. It was time to be on with the trip. It wasn't heroic, it wasn't dangerous, this trip. But just then I felt that it was, and I certainly felt a pressure to find out. But what work, dragging an unaccustomed pack in the noon sun. I looked dubiously at my map to make sure I was heading toward Karyes. (I was going to the capital of Athos to present my papers, and to get the paper which would permit me free entrance to the monasteries.) I found myself sweating, sitting down regularly, nibbling already on my cheese. Worst of all, cursing the narrow stone walk I was climbing. Athos was intentionally hard to travel. It would have been hard enough for a mule, let alone a man burdened like a mule.

I felt alone in nature again, shortly after starting out. The landscape I had seen in the morning became the whole world along the steep path up from Dafne to the ridge where Karyes lies. Now there were trees too. Many evergreens, but also beech and elm and high laurel bushes, not yet blooming. The path was heavy in shade, and it was only occasionally that I got a view down onto the never far ocean, oily blue in the sun. Nature was embracing.

Until, after three hours during which I had seen nothing human except an occasional monk passing on a donkey, I came suddenly to a view of Karyes in the next valley. It was a simple town in its way, but a real capital in the Athian sense. The cathedral for the whole peninsula was there, and the main administration building of the independent republic; there was a hotel, and more shops and restaurants than I had seen in Dafne. There were several streets, a number of private houses, a few independent monastic organizations. Here was the heart of Athos. I felt it at once. Even from the hill at a distance.

Yet I was too tired to feel much more that day. It was near sundown. I hurried to present my papers and to find myself a room and a meal. I went right out to the guest room of the monastery of Koutloumousi, a quarter of an hour from Karyes. From there I had my first clear view of the peak of Mount Athos. There is snow on it almost all year round, and in that clear dusk the mountain glistened against the sky at the south end of the peninsula. My feelings were carried back to the pitch of excitement they had reached when I landed at Dafne. But this evening it was different. This mountain reaching into the sky seemed to be asking my own growing question: where did nature merge with the supernatural here? I took that question to sleep with me.

On the entire trip from Hierissos to Karyes my senses were occupied by scenes of external nature. I felt the spontaneity, directness, and innocence of that nature much more than usual. And yet I knew: the principle of human life on Athos was devotion to the supernatural. To an unseen, inward realm, which is without change or place, and which rules and judges the world.

Man's effort to communicate with the divine is incessant. And only communicants can judge whether the effort is effective. Many of these, of course, have made the judgment "yes." But I have seldom been more impressed by the decisiveness of such a judgment than I was at the monastery of Pantocrator (the all-ruling one), where I spent Saturday night and Easter Sunday morning.

A lucky accident had taken me to Pantocrator. I left Karyes Saturday morning with the intention of going to Vatopedi, a large, wealthy monastery on the coast northeast of Karyes. The walk was hard, the paths unclearly marked, and by early afternoon I was worn out. Through the bushes, unexpectedly, I saw what looked like a mediaeval castle, with a military tower at one end, a rampart leading up to it, and an impregnable location on a cliff over the sea. There were rows of balcony rooms, propped up on stilts, all around the top of the building. Showing through from the courtyard were the blood-red Byzantine cupolas of the church. This was Pantocrator. I was fascinated and went to it.

From the caïque and from my Friday walk I had already seen four monasteries. I understood the kind of impression they made. All were built in the high or late middle ages: from the tenth to the fifteenth centuries. Originally they were fortified castles. Therefore these monasteries were not built close to the ground. Typically they were built directly into a cliff, so that the lowest stories of the monastery itself were already quite high; often fifty feet, I think. This inaccessibility was what the monks wanted as a symbol of their spiritual schism from the outer world. The same motive governed the choice of a location for their buildings: one is on a cliff over the sea; another in the high-walled cleft of a valley; a third at the summit of a rocky hill. Seen from a distance the monasteries look like huge natural growths.

Pantocrator occupied the first kind of location: a cliff over the sea. I climbed down from the hill, through more brush, and walked quickly to the monastery. Climbed the winding ramp entrance over the moat, and went into the courtyard. It was about three in the afternoon. The place was all mine, empty. Finally I found a man working in a dark corner. I told him that I wanted to go to the guest room—every monastery has one, where free lodging is provided for travellers—to put down my things and rest. He pointed the way. I went, and found the door locked. No one in sight. I went back to him again and asked where the monks were. Oh, they are having a nap. Wait a half hour. They need to sleep now because they will be up all night for the Easter mass. During the following two and a half hours of waiting I absorbed the deep afternoon mood of the monastery courtyard.

I was caught entirely into the harmony and peace of that scene. The church was the focus of the courtyard, the sanctuary protected by the high walls which met each other at odd angles. The monks' quarters, the kitchen, and the various work- and storerooms were built into the walls, and surrounded the court. Three stories high. Each story presented an arched corridor toward the court, with the rooms behind it. To me, the effect of such arches and of the general roundness of Byzantine churches has always been pacifying; the opposite of the Gothic effect. There was other peace too. In a corner of the yard a large, blossoming cherry tree was shedding its petals onto the worn stone floor of the court. Such stillness. Rather I should say it was so loud that it was intensely still. For the sea was pouring and rolling against the cliff below us; but as is the way with seas, this Aegean roar was quickly absorbed into the subconscious, where it raged silently. A peacefully violent background. (In fact, it was only accidentally that I had even noticed the water. I had turned my head sleepily to the east, and there, through a little arch, I had noticed the Aegean.) An enormous gray-blue plain extending unbounded, or nearly; the dark outline of the island of Thasos was faintly visible out there. As light as a suspended thought, like Amouliane the day before.

Around five-thirty a few monks began to appear. One of them, appointed as master of guest friendship, took me to my room. Four simple beds, without sheets, a dirty floor, cold: but I was glad to be there. I was left alone a few minutes, then called to coffee. Every new arrival in the monasteries is given coffee, often with a sweet, and a little glass of *ouzo* or raki. It was all served in the kitchen.

A rather violent wood fire heated my cup of Turkish coffee, and

I sat down to talk with the guestmaster and another monk. Greek curiosity: Where was I from? What did I do, know, read, like? I asked questions too. And got answers. There were only fifteen monks in Pantocrator. Young men weren't coming any more. Decline of spiritual life. It was hard living in a monastery. And much more.

The time went, the sun set, and I was given dinner at last. This was fasting time, though, in fact the summit of the fasting which had been going on for weeks at Athos. I had good dark wine, a bowl of cold macaroni, some dark bread and cheese to go with it. That was all the food or talk for the time. The two monks had been curious, but they were in no intimate mood. In them, as in many of the acquaintances I made on Athos, I found a basic reserve, even distance. Certainly none of the formal pleasantness which the lay world is accustomed to. The mood of these monks was more essential.

I left them and went straight to bed: the fifteen monks straight to church. They would spend the whole night at mass, and I only from midnight on: fine. I slept hard for six hours, curled under my clothes, coat, scarf, and four blankets. Then the knock: I thanked the knocker and went back to sleep. Violently, heavily. To be awakened in about a half-hour by an uncanny cacophony which I expect never to forget. The first noise was from firecrackers. Then the steady ringing of a bell interrupted—or competed against—by the noise of metal being hammered by sticks. Which gave off a dull, melancholy sound: the joy of bell noise woven with the weird dismay of the wood-beaten metal drove me out of bed.

I looked out on the courtyard. The church was bright with candlelight: a point of flame in each window. Otherwise the night was tar-black. I went directly to the church, was escorted into the sub-cupola room, and seated—rather stood up—in one of the wooden high-chairs-with-a-narrow-seat which line the walls of Greek churches. I was right in the middle of things. From sleep to this mysterious interior was a bewildering transition.

There were only fifteen monks at Pantocrator, but all were participating. Two were chanting at left-centre; two busy behind the iconostasis; two chanting at right-front out of my sight. And they kept moving. Bringing an icon to be kissed in the nave; bringing a lectern and two huge candlesticks; or bringing a jewelled Bible to be set on a stand. I was impressed by the vital, compelling way these monks employed the limited space they had. They were actors during their mass. In the middle of their act I was placed. And stayed for two and a half hours, until I was bleary.

While I was there I criticized and praised. Had I the right to my own opinion about this sacred scene, which I was permitted to see, and to which I came as an outsider? I hope so.

Let me say that I raised my own cry during parts of the liturgy: it was "human, all too human." I raised it when I saw the carelessness of the performance, first. The forgetting of lines, the confusion about which monk was to sing or read at a certain time, the chattering of monks off stage. Just a routine to be gone through. I raised my cry again when I saw my special host of the afternoon appear from the altar in an elegant yellow robe. I thought of the contrast between the black daily robes of all the monks and the splendor of their costumes this evening. A show, a performance! And all this incense, what was it really? Burning, narcotic spice. And these icons which were repeatedly kissed. Fairly crude paintings. A whole series of reductions occurred to me.

Yet I was surprised to find myself countering all these feelings: not by destroying them, but by saying, "yes, but." But what a tremendous, courageous voice was being lifted here into the skies! Over and over, in all the mixture of despair and joy which Byzantine hymns incarnate, over and over it was sung: "Christ has risen, out of the dead," Christ has risen for the salvation of man to the end of time. It was hard to raise this cry from dusk to dawn: but it was still being lifted with strength. If these were men, and just men, the most wonderful of animals, their cry was the more courageous. And that they should have gathered here, for this purpose, on this lonely cliff of the world, throughout this night: that seemed miraculous in itself.

And as I was thinking this I became aware, gradually, of an external event which seemed almost a symbolic counterpart of the miracle in the church. An orange-rose light was slowly filtering through the eastern windows of the church. It was the first hint of dawn. Around me the candles seemed less alone in the dark, the murals on the walls began to look less austere, and warmer, the strictness of the bearded faces grew milder. This half-dawn must have been increasing about us for some time, but I had become only gradually aware of it. The mass went on.

As it neared its end, though, I began to sense what would happen; what in fact did happen. The end of the mass, the moment when Resurrection was finally re-enacted in its human imitation, coincided with the fulness of sunrise. Out over the sea, beyond Thasos, the blinding globe had once more appeared over the ocean's rim. The whole monastery court and walls were transformed. Even to my eyes the moment was visionary. Christ's Resurrection *was* this returning, reliving innocence and vitality of day. I saw the mass' perfection, its fulness, in the ancient beginning of day. Christ has risen!

These were the last articulate feelings I had at Pantocrator. The mass ended about four, and I went back to bed. Everyone was joyful; Christ had risen. Eternal life had been celebrated and assured, as far as possible, to the celebrators. This was Pantocrator.

As I think back on it and what I experienced there, it seems the most significant moment of my trip to Athos. I keep coming back to the relation of the natural to the supernatural. Weren't these mere men who had acted before me? Men who had napped in the afternoon, put on fine robes at dusk, and chanted until dawn; all this they certainly were. What more were they? Why should they have been more? As it is, the finest of animals, raising a superb strenuous cry from the being's longing and dread, as it is they were much and enough. So I felt, at least. And I remain content to think of them as no more.

But not only the character of the men and their mass had strengthened my feeling. When I had first seen Pantocrator from the hill I had thought that it was almost a natural growth. Set on a cliff of the sea like a huge, complex geological eruption. (I remembered Goethe's thought that religion is nature's attempt to heal a wound in itself.) Later in the courtyard I had felt the harmony of being which dominated at Pantocrator: the soul and the body were happily together here, I had thought. Nature was all. Ambient, pure, and warm in the ever returning flood of the dawning sun.

Ultimately, the wealth of human souls is the main item in the Athian economy. Under black cloaks and beards, through a quite foreign language, in a very foreign spiritual environment, and in a short time, I found a number of friendly souls on Athos.

The most sympathetic person I met—I shall call him *K*—was a monk who had greeted me in Karyes, the night of my arrival there. I had gone to the post office to look for mail. Already I had begun to feel like a displaced person, and would gladly have found a letter from "beyond." (There was none there.) Perhaps it was this mood that made me especially grateful for *K*'s cheerful "comment

allez-vous?" The post office was dark and small; and letterless for me. I had felt at the end of the world. And then there came the promise of a human meeting.

The first trait I noticed in *K* was his pure directness. Perhaps it was the immediacy of his deepest being, his freedom from superficialities, which gave him this trait. At any rate, I met his essence before I noticed what body it was in. Not that the body was usual looking, particularly in the Athian context. *K* was around thirty-five and looked younger. A stocky, fiery-eyed, red-haired and red-bearded young monk. With a kind of grave-hilarious face, and a strenuous manner. He might have been Irish, to first sight.

We warmed to each other quickly. Athian friendships, I believe, often form that way. Little time was wasted on preparations for acquaintance. It seemed to us both that we should talk, and so *K* invited me to his cell. I accepted. We made our way promptly out into Karyes, walked across the dusky town, chatted in passing with an occasional busy monk, and in ten minutes reached *K*'s own home.

He lived in a single, comfortable room in a Russian monastery on a hilltop over Karyes. The building itself was a sad relic of past glory. Where there had previously been two hundred monks, there were now two. Once the corridors had been lined with elegant private chapels, but now the whole interior of the monastery was filthy, broken-down, and neglected. The wooden stairs by which we entered were rotting. Lack of money and the dearth of monks from post-Revolutionary Russia were the causes of the decay.

Yet in this setting we had no trouble making ourselves comfortable. *K*'s small room was attractive. He offered me a wicker chair, and banana liqueur, and sat down himself in his straight desk chair. From where we sat we could look out toward the glistening peak of Mount Athos, and down onto calm Karyes. And there we talked.

It was a rare, deep moment for me, sharing this man's spiritual environment and being.

Our talk flowed out of the situation. *K* began by telling me that his main activity was participation in mass. This job took time and strength. As the Cathedral of Karyes was close to his cell, he was able to go there often and easily. It was my impression, as we talked, that *K* looked on the Cathedral almost as a second home: an intimate, known sanctuary.

By profession he was a painter. Every Athos monk who doesn't live in a monastery has to support himself: by his art, handicraft, weaving, farming, or other work. *K* did this by selling his very competent portraits and painted cards. Most of these he sent to foreign countries: and from them got a small income. It sufficed for him, I gathered; and he was anxious, in any case, to keep money from becoming an end of his art. He permitted his art itself, in fact, only on the condition of its harmonizing completely with his religious life. And wanted his painting to emerge from the same springs as his devotion. I think that *K* would have cut off his means of support instantly, if he had felt it was interfering with his piety.

In his remarks about art—as always, I suspect—*K* was direct and open. With the kind of unified, uncompromising vision which religious people sometimes attain. I saw this vision in his ideas about history, too, especially about the conflict between Christianity and Communism. *K* saw this conflict as disastrous, by temporal measurements. Like many monks on Athos he was sure that his holy peninsula was doomed, and would become a sacrifice to the conflict of cultures. But he interpreted the whole pattern of history as— essentially—a spectacle projected from God's providential mind. On that scale, he insisted, the present crisis had meaning, and would be redeemed. *K* trusted divine providence more than most men trust the sequence of day and night.

Throughout the long talk—two or three hours—which these lines suggest, we had been sitting in *K*'s cell. The sun had set, and my friend had lighted candles. Outside it had grown dark: a few echoing candles formed points of light down below in the town. Around us on the walls of the room hung *K*'s paintings—of monasteries, long-bearded friends, the sea—and his few books were arranged on the table. There was something deceptively *gemütlich* in the occasion; as though we might be two scholars meeting in a university study.

Yet I remember exactly what broke that illusion. There was a sudden bursting forth of bells. The night's mass was startlingly announced. *K* was being called. In a way it was odd to me. This man whom I had felt so quickly close to was to answer now to an ultimate call which didn't reach me. It seemed hard to decapitate our conversation in this way. *K* got up and reached for his black cloak and hood.

But we weren't really to part. I should have known. First *K* offered me his room for the night; he would be away until dawn. I accepted. Then I—feeling growing shame at my sleepfulness—asked him to wake me at midnight and to bring me down to the Cathedral to see the mass: it would begin to reach one of its several climaxes at that time. He agreed. We weren't really parting, when he left in his black cloak.

At midnight the door opened: I woke hard, having at first no idea where I was. There stood *K,* elated from mass, his face almost fiery, shining from dew and joy. I leaped out of bed—all dressed—and followed him, as I slowly came back to consciousness. *K* led the way quickly down the stone path, holding a flickering, insufficient candle before us. A chilly, virginal night which woke me up shockingly. And then soon, from this night, as quickly as we had entered it, we plunged into the full, chant-full, incense-heavy Cathedral. I took my candle and stood there, until the procession began to form. From sleep to this interior was a shock; the church hung like a dream over my amazed vision.

K's presence, though, kept me in touch with reality. For though he was responding, no doubt much more deeply than I, to the scene, he helped me to feel like an authentic participant. By asking whether I didn't admire this or that stage of the liturgy; or by explaining the singing in an enthusiastic whisper. His spiritual enthusiasm and openness made the event real for me. The hours until dawn passed in extraordinary fascination.

We had little chance for more talk after the mass. *K* was tired, and we both wanted sleep. He went off to another room of his monastery, to bed, leaving me in his room. And though we met and talked again in the morning, we knew that the centre of our encounter was behind us. It will be remembered for a long time.

When I think of that man it is of a radiant point of spiritual enthusiasm and openness. I appeared on his horizon at the peak moment in his spirit's year. He welcomed me, and gave his being bountifully to me. And so offered a warm and meaningful introduction to Athos. Few others could have done it.

The second portrait is brief and slight. As I left Vatopedi—the next monastery beyond Pantocrator—by mule I was accompanied for two hours by a young monk. He had business in Karyes, and was, I think, glad of company. At first I had thought he was a girl —one of those French *dames* who are occasionally, it is said, sneaked onto the peninsula. He had flowing, ruddy hair; soft, moulded features; and delicate movements. There was something strong about him, though. (As there generally was about the not too uncommon effeminate monks whom I saw at Athos.) I liked him.

On the ride we talked some. He told me he was from Crete. He
was eighteen. And why had he come: or was that too difficult a
question? Not difficult. He had a cousin on Athos. And he—my
companion—had liked it there immediately. What did he do here
now? He went to school. At Karyes there is a regular Greek Gymnasium for novice monks. The school is staffed by lay teachers, like
any Greek public school. We talked on about such things at our
leisure. He was charmingly pleased with life, and with Athos. It
had been a characteristically pleasant Athian encounter.

But it left me with a characteristically serious reflection. It
seemed terribly arbitrary for this boy to have come to Athos. How
could he have even partly known what a commitment he was making? Or what he was sacrificing or gaining? I felt this same distress
for a number of young men I saw and met on the holy mountain.

The third portrait is the most difficult to sketch. Father *T*—the
name I will give this strong, sixty-five–year–old monk—entered
my life at the monastery of Lavra. I had gone there several days
after Pantocrator. And was looking at the monks' ancient dining
hall, preparing myself to go on to Kavsokalubia. Lavra was already
fairly near the southern end of the peninsula; my next walk was to
take me over very rough ground nearly to the point. I saw Father *T*
near me, and asked him about the route.

He explained all its difficulties in a rather amused way. I began
to imagine that I would never find the paths. Until he said, casually, "I'll go with you." I was astonished. He'd just given me such
a long description of the route.

I sat down to wait for him to prepare his bags. In a few minutes
he appeared, and called me to his cell: a bit of refreshment before
the trip. The cell was pleasant: a tidy, bare, bachelor apartment,
with two small rooms and a tiny chapel. But it was not appointed

for guests, and we sat in the kitchen. There we had good *ouzo*, coffee, and *loukoumi*. I asked him why he wanted to go to Kavsokalubia. (The beginning of that inquest.) He had to be in Karyes in three days, and would get the boat from Kavsokalubia. So he said. But he was going the wrong direction for Karyes. As I saw him bustling around, filling his woolen shoulder bag with clothes, I came to the conclusion that he was anxious to make a trip. And indeed that was true. (Although I know that he also wanted to show me the road.) Getting out of his home monastery onto the paths of Athos was exciting to Father *T*.

We left Lavra shortly after noon at a good pace. I was delighted to have company for this walk: we presumed it would take about three hours. A hard grind alone. Hard anyway on the paths of Athos. This path was especially narrow, simply a bed of stones laid at odd angles, often vertically, and winding up and down over the rocky hills. The landscape was still that of the first morning on the boat. Austere and dry: that day even the incessant sea, down below us, looked dry.

From time to time we rested; at a spring, or on a cold rock. Then I began to realize that Father *T* was delighted with my company. We had not talked much. But he was a lonely man, excited by an expedition with a visitor from the outside world. He had a fine smile, mercurial and almost gleeful. I looked at him closely. A wry, applelike face, a Vermont farmer. Stringy, gray-black hair. Live eyes. His hands were remarkable too. Very strong and wiry. I had noticed that he was enduring the hike better than I.

During these pauses he usually propagandized rather sweetly—as though knowing it was no use—for his faith. He had only the most rudimentary ideas about other branches of Christianity: the difference between Catholicism and Protestantism was unfamiliar to him—as, I think, to most Athos monks. But he asked me when we, in the West, would return to the Greek church, our true mother. Why had we strayed so far? At another pause he told me about the Second Coming. He expected Christ to return in 1968, in some form, probably as the cause of a huge punitive war to cleanse man's sins. I was surprised to encounter these ideas on Athos: but I learned later that they are common there. Or at another pause, as we sat looking up at a small hut, perched high on a cliff, he told me about the miracle which had once happened there. In fact, as I gathered, to him the whole ground of Athos was holy: countless miracles had happened; here, over there, down in the valley: the whole land was a symbol. For what? For the goodness and love of the Virgin Mary, the patroness of Athos. (Appropriate for a peninsula of men.) Athos is paradise, said Father T. And yet I repeat: there was something wonderfully sweet in his manner of telling me all this; as though he half believed it might help me, yet was resigned to my impregnability.

By various stages, then, we approached our destination. Kavsokalubia is the first of the so-called sketes which I visited. A skete is a community of monks who live together in a small village in complete independence: there are some six sketes on Athos. The extraordinary character of Kavsokalubia is that its monk citizens—about fifty now—are all artists. They live in a cleft between high hills, against the back of a valley, under the peak of Mount Athos itself, and facing the objectless, limitless-looking Aegean. Father T and I came suddenly, over the brink of a hill, onto this community.

It was then that I was to discover anew my good luck in meeting with Father T. For he was genuinely anxious to have me get an impression of Kavsokalubia. He knew everyone there: whether in every case as real acquaintances or simply as brothers in Christ. And he proceeded, systematically, to take me on a visit to the houses and the ateliers of the main artists. It was hard work: more up and down; attempts to make conversation; a glass of *ouzo* in every house until both Father *T* and I fairly ricocheted back the stony path to the guesthouse at dusk. There was something hilarious about the situation, I decided; and I was never sure whether Father *T* saw it that way. I didn't understand him well. But I knew that through some lively Christian motive he had done me good service in Kavsokalubia.

I saw this man for the last time the next afternoon. We were in the same boat which was taking us to different destinations; me to another skete, him on toward his mission in Karyes. I left him with real feeling, as I disembarked at Agia Anna. He had been a sweet, vital, unexpected friend. The kind of accident which I had hoped for at Athos. And he left me with that kind of manly parting I had come to expect there. The mood of it was: it was good that we met; but our parting is no cause for sentiment; we will be rejoined soon in a happier and purer world. Did he really know that I would be in the other department of that world?

The last portrait is a group portrait, of the artist monks whom I met at Kavsokalubia, on my tour with Father *T*. I have described the geographical situation of that skete. You have to climb or descend in order to go anywhere. The houses are all at different levels on the hillside; from a distance the effect is that of an enormous chessboard with pieces scattered randomly over it. The pieces, the houses, are very attractive; the most comfortable quarters I saw anywhere on Athos. Two-story stucco houses, each with its own small church, and with ample room. The roominess is easily explained: at Kavsokalubia the number of monks has diminished by more than half in the last decade.

In each house live at least two monks; often more. One of them,

if there are two, is the *hierontas,* the father; the other the *hypotak-tikos,* the servant. This is the arrangement in all the sketes. In Kav-sokalubia this system results in one monk being the master painter, the other being the apprentice. The two live and work closely to-gether in the church of their house. I imagine that this union of church, home, and atelier under one roof can be an especially ex-citing environment for a creative life. Though I doubt that it often is.

My portrait of these monks themselves has to be sketchy. I had the general impression that they were not important artists, but that they were joyful artists. Their art itself was exclusively icon paint-ing, except for a few who do small woodcarved icons. A frequent tactic of this painting, I learned from the monks concerned, was to choose a model in Byzantine painting and to copy it. One of these painters, to my mind the best, said that he felt weak unless he had such a prototype. The result of this copying, it seemed to me, was a watering down of the austerity and depth of Byzantine icons. An-other result, obviously, was that the subjects of the paintings were limited: to Christ, the Virgin, and a restricted number of saints. It was uncanny to see the assiduous attempt of these painters to work today in the frozen style of the fifteenth century. There was a rea-son, though; these painters, as they said, were certain that this de-votional style was the most pleasing to God.

Here lay the source of their joy. In the conviction that their art was of the highest spiritual importance. Their lives were whole. Prayer and painting were parts of a single devotional thrust.

Their joy was clear enough on their faces. A beard does much to beautify a face; but it alone cannot make a face look joyful. (I saw a few old beard-faces at Athos which were twisted and tired. Not many, though.) Two of the master painters I talked with were old men. They had fine white beards, and a good deal of patriarchal mellowness. They seemed to me among the most broadly human people I met at Athos. Much curiosity about America; they send many of their paintings there, on order from Greek churches in Baltimore, New York . . . Two of the *hypotaktikoi* were also sympathetic: imaginative, delicate people with a great devotion to their work. They all treated me with friendliness, and I left thoroughly pleased with their community.

I left with some emotion, too, as I had left Pantocrator. For I was astonished, partly, simply at the existence of such a place. Yet in addition I felt a certain rightness about Kavsokalubia. The wholeness of the artistic lives led there was exemplary, or seemed so. There art and joy seemed to have found one another and to have chosen marriage.

After leaving Father *T* in the boat, I made my last visit on Athos: to the skete of Agia Anna, the mother of Mary. This village resembles Kavsokalubia in many ways. It is built on the side of a hill; has some forty or fifty houses, each with its own church; and is inhabited primarily by icon painters and by weavers. Only the village structure is conspicuously different at Anna. The houses there are far apart, and interhouse communication is steep and hard. I had the feeling that Anna was the most austere spiritual centre on the peninsula.

But I will not take the leisure here to report fully: on the revered foot of Anna; on the tree-trunk beds where saints of a stronger day slept; or on the incessant night masses held in different private chapels throughout the community. In discussing Anna, as in reporting on almost any settlement I saw on Athos, I could introduce curious and detailed personal observations. So much on

Athos was new and extraordinary to me. Yet I have been trying to focus my interest on the general.

So I prefer to call up only one more Athian experience; one of my last, and most significant. Yet though it happened at Agia Anna I doubt that the source of the experience was divine. In any case, its result stirred.

It was at dusk, ten days after my arrival at Athos, my last night there. I was alone for the evening, and was sitting looking west to the still sea, and east toward Mount Athos. After the constant pressure, interest, and effort of the recent days it was fine to be quiet and alone.

In a mood of almost exalted peace I had what seemed a sudden creative awareness of the unity of my recent experiences. The mood had this shape. The first stars were appearing in the mild sky; there was a thin slice of moon; the sea was still, and held a slight glow of redness from the gone sun; and behind, always there, the hills of rocky Athos were the background. In this absolute unity of nature's peace, in this pure ambience of nature, Saint Anna's skete spread around me. Here and there a candle burned in a window. The skete was at rest. And as part of the peace of nature it seemed a harmonious element in the calmness which joined me to that seen moon up there, to the still sea, and to the mountains. Which joined me to the creative and created, bearing and dying temporal world. Briefly: which made all multiplicity one.

Then gradually, almost of themselves, all the other elements of my experience of Athos was gathered into this mood. The great monasteries, with their restlessly praying monks; Father *T*, my painter friend in Karyes, and the chestnut-haired boy at Vatopedi; the painters at Kavsokalubia; the sea I sailed in order to reach Athos and the hills I had climbed on it—all these parts of a universe were parts of the scene I had in vision that night. They were all out there, not very far from me. They were all under the moon, and under the stars: they had all been made and would be unmade. I knew them and loved them for it. And for the deep, restless protest which the Athian monks raised against this knowledge.

Postword: Gevgelija Again

It seemed years, almost a lifetime, since I had been in Gevgelija. This time the train, which I had taken in Salonika that morning, carried me to the border stations. On the Greek side we had all stepped out to stretch and to show documents. There were few formalities. I walked back and forth beside the train for ten minutes, remembering how beautiful Salonika had been that morning, and how I had loved my first bath and shave after Athos. Salonika was in any case, for me, a city of the senses. In my part of a night there, on this return, I had gone down to that sea, and walked among the people. Still, after Syra or Smyrna, Salonika seemed the most sensuously *there*. And unchangeable. Now, this morning, I had to face departure from all this.

I strolled past the Greek customs-house and looked in. There were a couple of the men whose vitality had welcomed me to Hellas on a not yet forgotten morning. They were busy and joking. Beyond them I saw the door into the restaurant, which on that day had seemed so Rabelaisian. What artichokes! But perhaps it would no longer be so exciting, it occurred to me. The contrast with Jugoslavia had been massive.

I guess it still was. We soon got back on the train, crossed the famous border, and squeaked to a stop a few hundred yards farther on, at the Jugoslavian station. God, how familiar it was! The air was businesslike, not like that in the rundown Balkan shack which separated Italy from Jugoslavia. But how miserable this business-likeness was. Brisk, soulless, lost. Catching myself muttering, I realized to what degree my prejudices had the better of me.

We were soon, in any case, far into the land. The wheels ground, the smoke poured past the window in tatters, and what had first been mountains began dropping off to the long plains south of Skopje. I settled into the corner of our filled compartment and tried to read. It was no use. A fat man had pulled a cigar on us. I went choking into the corridor, where the air was hard and coaly. It was almost time for dinner.

As I bent over at the window a Greek couple squeezed past. They were talking rapidly, and on something personal. I paid no attention. I saw them later in the diner, trying to get Greek foods. They were good-looking, probably in their mid-thirties. On their way to Munich. Full of life.

Even now I am not quite sure what they did to propose themselves into these last words. I have absolutely nothing dramatic to recount of them. I never spoke with them, never knew their names. I only saw them, in a rather full sense of that activity.

For the last time in this life (probably) I saw them in the Munich train station. Our trip through Jugoslavia was over. I had passed them a few times in the corridor, and been able to exchange something knowing, by smile, as though we had all realized our difference from the Jugoslavian businessmen and soldiers who were hemming us in. There had been some affinities.

Then had come Munich, another world. Neon signs, Western

alphabet; The West. We had all started off through the train station into our respective versions of the twentieth century. The pressure of our time, with all its weight. I felt unaccountably moved by
meaning, and sunken in on myself.

As I started down the street away from the *Bahnhof,* I looked
back. There, just emerging into this new world, was the Greek
couple. They smiled, waving. It was the good Greek wave, with
fingers rhythmically drawn in to the palm, then opened out. It was
a fraught farewell. I waved back.

INDEX

Lightning Source UK Ltd.
Milton Keynes UK
UKOW04f0828041215

264014UK00003B/83/P